RISE BEYOND ORDINARY STUDY GUIDE

Rise Beyond Ordinary Study Guide

PETE ROBERTSON

SET FREE

Contents

Published by Set Free Press
Copyright © 2025 by Pete Robertson
First Printing, 2025

First Printing, 2025
Printed in the United States of America

To Order Additional Copies of this resource, you may order online at www.risebeyondordinary.com

ISBN/SKU 979-8-9901733-4-7

What to Expect

Rise Beyond Ordinary and Unlock a Spiritual Revolution
When we Rise Beyond Ordinary, we unlock a spiritual revolution— a transformative movement within us that unleashes untapped potential and brings forth a powerful change. This is a shift in your calling that elevates you beyond the average, surpassing common expectations. As you step out of routines that produce minimal fruit, you break free from limitations and embrace a higher calling, achieving more in your thinking and living.

As Jesus calls us to live differently, we begin to rise above mediocrity and reach for something extraordinary. Your life, influenced by His truth, becomes a testament to a higher level of purpose and impact. Matthew 28:19-20 commissions us to make disciples of all nations, and in doing so, we see our own lives transformed and elevated to fulfill God's greater plan.

Being a disciple of Jesus empowers us to pursue greatness, striving to become more than the world expects, with the Holy Spirit as our guide. A true disciple by God's grace seeks God's will and embraces a higher calling—one that leads to deeper spiritual growth, greater impact, and a life of fulfillment beyond our wildest dreams. Our awakening begins when we start discipling others, who, in turn, disciple others. In doing so, we become part of a movement that changes the world and makes history, one disciple at a time. *2 Timothy 2:2* reminds us, *"And the things you have heard me say in the presence of many witnesses entrust to reliable people who will also be qualified to teach others."* This is how we rise beyond the ordinary—by embracing our divine calling and sharing it with others who long for the same transformative lifestyle.

There are countless books on discipleship, and while this one shares some of the same principles as others, it offers something uniquely powerful. This book reveals a proven strategy established by Jesus with His disciples—a strategy that saw His message spread rapidly across the world in a short time. You will learn how to apply this same approach in your own life and ministry. You will discover why His movement exploded and hear inspiring stories of others who are living out Jesus' teachings, seeing their ministries flourish globally.

This book is for disciples who are ready to take their ministries to the next level and are committed to making history. Jesus did not call us to be weak, but strong and courageous, with a mission to advance His Kingdom—one disciple at a time.

I created this interactive workbook to complement Rise Beyond Ordinary Book, designed for both individual reflection and small group discussion. The study guide follows the first eight chapters of the book and is structured as an 8-week journey. While the full book contains 12 chapters and offers much deeper context, the workbook focuses on key highlights from the first eight. For the richest experience, I highly recommend reading each chapter in the book before working through the corresponding section in the guide.

The study guide is flexible and can be used for daily personal reflection, in a small group setting, or as a one-on-one discipleship tool. I highly encourage you to go through the entire study—it will help you deeply absorb and apply the teachings from the book.

To enhance your experience, you also have access to an 8-week video series that is designed to support your personal journey or serve as a weekly resource for group discussions. Visit www.risebeyondordinary.com to view videos.

What to expect Personal Study:

To get the most out of your daily personal study, begin by reading the corresponding chapter from the book first. This provides the context you will need to reflect deeply and answer the questions thoughtfully. While the study guide focuses on the first eight chapters—each divided into five sections for daily reflection—the book also includes four additional training chapters to further equip you.

The book itself takes about 20 to 25 minutes to read each chapter, while the study guide will take around 15 to 20 minutes a day to complete for 5 days. As you work through both the book and the study, your perspective on the world around you will begin to shift. You will be deeply blessed and challenged—and if you put into practice what you learn, you will experience a transformed life, filled with God's love and empowered by a personal ministry that can truly turn the world upside down.

Do not make this just another religious exercise you rush through to check off your list. This study is different—it is life-changing. Slow down. Always begin each day in prayer, inviting the Holy Spirit to open your heart and reveal what He wants you to see. As you work through the questions, approach them with honesty, vulnerability, and humility. Let the Holy Spirit lead you, shape you, and bring lasting transformation throughout your journey.

What to expect small group Study:

To use this study in a small group setting, it is important that you still complete the work as if you were doing it for personal study. However, when preparing for group discussion, highlight key questions or sections in the book that stand out to you. This will not only help you reflect more deeply on what God is revealing to you, but it will also enrich your group discussion by offering insights that may help others see things from a new perspective.

What to expect One-on-One discipleship:

This study can be a powerful tool for one-on-one discipleship when used in a way that promotes conversation over presentation. You and your disciple should read through one chapter of the book each week, highlighting and discussing the key insights that stand out. Then, when you meet up, go through the study guide together reading each section out loud and sharing your answers honestly and vulnerably.

In my book "Keys to Being Set Free", each section is structured with a "coach read" and "student read" format. The same approach can be applied here. Most days include three key highlights—take turns reading each one aloud and use them as a springboard for deeper discussion. As you read together out loud and answer the questions, allow the Holy Spirit to guide your conversation, and focus on what He wants to reveal.

Continue working through each day of the study guide chapter until your meeting time ends. Simply mark your spot and pick up where you left off at your next session. With about an hour to an hour and a half per meeting, plan to spend at least two weeks on each chapter. Completing all 8 chapters will take approximately 16 weeks. Be sure to cast vision with your disciples before you begin, so they understand the purpose and journey ahead.

When you meet, choose a quiet, distraction-free environment that allows for genuine connection, spiritual growth, and the freedom for the Holy Spirit to move. If you are meeting over Zoom or other online platforms, the same principle applies—both you and your disciple should be in a space that is free from distractions.

Before you begin discipling someone, be sure you are personally living out the principles taught in this book. Most importantly, make sure your disciple is F.A.T.—Faithful, Available, and Teachable. Cast a clear vision, set expectations early, and raise the bar high. Within the first month of meeting, your disciple should be preparing to disciple someone else—even while continuing to meet with you. This is the key to multiplying yourself. Whether using this study or another discipleship resource, true multiplication happens when every disciple you invest in is also actively investing in someone else.

If you need additional materials, download the Natural Discipleship App in the app store and explore the "9 Steps" or "Keys to Being Set Free" curriculum, both are free and are transferable.

Rise Beyond Ordinary Study Guide

Rise Beyond Ordinary
♫ ♫ **Scan the QR code to listen.**
Album can be streamed on Apple Music, Amazon Music, Spotify and other listening platforms.

**https://youtu.be/
YzgPg1VKys0**

Chapter 1

Session 1 Casting Clear Vision

To get the most out of your daily personal study, begin by reading the corresponding chapter from the book. This provides the context you will need to reflect deeply and answer the questions thoughtfully. While the study guide focuses on the first eight chapters—each divided into five sections for daily reflection—the book also includes four additional training chapters to further equip you.

Start each day in prayer, inviting the Holy Spirit to open your heart and show you what He wants you to see. As you work through the questions, do so with honesty, vulnerability, and humility. Let the Holy Spirit lead you, shape you, and bring lasting transformation through this journey.

PERSONAL STUDY DAY 1

OVERVIEW:

Casting Vision chapter introduces the journey ahead, laying the foundation for your discipleship path. It emphasizes the importance of understanding the end goal—loving the world as Jesus did—before starting. A disciple must have a clear vision to fulfill their mission effectively, just as Jesus did. The book is designed to help you see people through Jesus' eyes, remove obstacles to intimacy with Him, and build a multiplying discipleship ministry. The goal is to equip you to disciple others, creating a chain of disciples that multiplies up to nine generations. The principles in this book have been tested globally, and as you apply them, you will be part of a movement that transforms lives, just like Gatungo, whose ministry spread across four countries in two years.

Proverbs 29:18 (KJV/NIV) "Where there is no vision, the people perish; but he that keeps the law, happy is he. Where there is no revelation, people cast off restraint; but blessed is the one who heeds wisdom's instruction."

PERSONAL APPLICATION

Key Highlight:

A disciple casts a clear vision for those they disciple. Without a sense of purpose and a vision of the end goal, we cannot expect disciples to fulfill their mission effectively. Jesus was a vision caster and so must we.

1. What does it mean to "cast a clear vision" for those you disciple, and how can you do that effectively?

2. What role does clarity of vision play in helping disciples remain committed and focused in their spiritual growth?

3. In what ways can a lack of vision or purpose hinder the effectiveness of discipleship?

<u>Key Highlight:</u>

The ultimate end goal? That we as disciples have intimacy with Jesus, love the world as He did, and provide a roadmap for multiplying disciples who disciple others! We will address the most significant question that every disciple will eventually ask: Why did Jesus come to this world and die on a cross for humanity? The answer is simple and memorable: Love (John 3:16). Jesus loved His disciples, and that love was passed on to others. This book is designed to help disciples see people the way Jesus sees them. I assure you that if you approach this journey with humility and an open heart, it will lead to a fruitful discipleship ministry that far exceeds your expectations.

4. What do you think it means to have true intimacy with Jesus? How is that reflected in your daily life?

5. Have I clearly defined the purpose and end goal of my discipleship journey? What should it look like?

6. What are some practical ways we can begin to see people the way Jesus sees them?

Key Highlight:

What does nine generations of disciples mean? It refers to a model of discipleship where your direct disciple goes on to disciple someone else, and their disciple disciples another person, and so on, extending up to nine generations or more deep. Each generation builds upon the previous one, creating a chain of discipleship that multiplies themselves.

This is how the early church exploded across the known world, and we will train you in all of this in the multiplication chapter. Consider the story of a servant leader named Gatungo. He embraced these principles, and in his own words, they transformed not only his life but also the ministry God was calling him to.

He learned to identify and eliminate the religious barriers that held him back, shifting his focus to the essential principle of drawing nearer to Jesus. This change ultimately led him to make disciples who, in turn, disciple others.

Within just two years of applying what he learned from the training, Gatungo has built an incredible network of disciples spanning four countries, with many of them forming five to nine generations of disciples.

7. What do you think was the key factor in Gatungo's ability to build such an incredible network of disciples in just two years?

8. How does the idea of forming multiple generations of disciples shape your understanding of long-term ministry goals?

PRAYER

Lord, as I begin this study, open my eyes to the vision You have for my discipleship journey. Help me to approach each question with humility and vulnerability, allowing the Holy Spirit to transform my heart and mind. Guide me in casting a clear vision for those I disciple and help me to live out Your love in practical ways. May my life reflect Your purpose, and may I multiply disciples who will continue this mission for generations to come. In Jesus' name, Amen.

DEEPER THOUGHT AND DISCUSSION

How does having a clear vision for multiplying disciples affect our willingness to invest in others for the long haul? How can we align our discipleship efforts with Jesus' vision for the harvest, and what steps can we take to ensure that vision shapes not only our actions but also the generations of disciples we aim to raise?

PERSONAL STUDY DAY 2

OVERVIEW:

The true cost of following Christ emphasizes that discipleship requires complete surrender and obedience to Jesus. According to Luke 14:27, following Christ means carrying our cross, which signifies a willingness to endure suffering and leave behind our old lives. Dietrich Bonhoeffer's book "The Cost of Discipleship" highlights that discipleship is not just about learning from Jesus but fully committing to Him, even to the point of suffering. Discipleship involves a steadfast commitment to following Jesus, aligning our lives with His teachings, and living for the Kingdom of God, not the world. This commitment shapes our journey, and true discipleship requires total surrender to God's will. By embracing this, disciples are empowered to make other disciples and live out the Kingdom values in their lives.

Isaiah 30:21 (NIV) "Whether you turn to the right or to the left, your ears will hear a voice behind you, saying, 'This is the way; walk in it.'".

PERSONAL APPLICATION:

<u>Key Highlight:</u>

Jesus makes this cost clear in Luke 14:27, stating, *"Whoever does not carry their cross and follow me cannot be my disciple."* By exploring this scripture, we will come to understand the profound commitment required to truly walk in His footsteps. In Dietrich Bonhoeffer's book The Cost of Discipleship, he emphasizes the paramount importance of obedience to the call of Christ. He said when Christ calls a man, he bids him come and die.

The cross means sharing the suffering of Christ to the last and to the fullest. He asserts that Jesus invites us to follow Him not merely as a teacher or a model for living a good life, but as the Christ, the Son of God. When Jesus calls us, there is an expectation that we approach Him with a clear understanding of His divine identity.

Bonhoeffer further explains that accepting this call requires us to leave behind our former lives in obedience to Christ. This relinquishment signifies a profound surrender, leading us into a new life filled with uncertainty, where we are no longer in control. It is in this space of submission that we begin to place our complete trust in God. Only a man that is totally committed in discipleship can experience the meaning of the cross. Suffering, then, is the badge of true discipleship. Living for Christ in a sin-filled world that often opposes righteousness will lead us to suffering. However, this suffering can serve to awaken our souls, allowing us to see Jesus in all His glory.

1. What does carrying your cross mean to you personally in your journey of discipleship? How have you experienced moments of sacrifice or suffering for Christ?

2. Reflecting on Dietrich Bonhoeffer's idea of "When Christ calls a man, he bids him come and die," what are some areas in your life where you need to fully surrender to God?

3. In what ways does living for Christ in today's world put us at odds with culture, and how should we respond to that tension?

<u>**Key Highlight:**</u>

If our lives do not reflect a genuine commitment to obedience and true discipleship, we must ask ourselves: how can we truly enter into communion with Christ? Can we even call ourselves disciples? Our actions—or lack thereof—may reveal a deeper disbelief in our calling. Without a complete surrender to His will at our conversion, our faith will remain weak, hindering our ability to become effective disciple makers.

Viewing our journey through this lens reveals that true discipleship is rooted in our willingness to wholeheartedly answer His call. As we embrace our identity as followers of Christ, let us strive to bear the fruits of the Spirit (Galatians 5:22-23) that lead us to the Tree of Life, reinforcing our commitment to live in accordance with His teachings and to reflect His love in a world in need of hope.

4. In what ways might a lack of obedience reveal disbelief or uncertainty in your calling as a disciple?

5. Can someone truly be a disciple of Jesus without living in daily obedience to Him? Why or why not?

<u>Key Highlight:</u>

Each day, as disciples of Christ, we are confronted with two paths: one that guides us toward the Tree of Life and another that leads us toward the Tree of Knowledge of Good and Evil (Gen 2:9-17). The choices we make on these paths shape our spiritual journey and relationship with God. In John 17:16, Jesus reminds us, *"They are not of the world, just as I am not of the world."* This powerful statement emphasizes that while we live in this world (Tree of Knowledge of good and evil), our ultimate allegiance lies with the Kingdom of God (Tree of Life). Our old life no longer exists; we now live only for the Kingdom of God.

Our new life is guided by our eyes fixed firmly on Jesus, allowing us to navigate the challenges around us without becoming entangled in them. While the temptation to focus on resolving worldly issues can be overwhelming, we must remember that Jesus is our ultimate fixer; it is no longer our responsibility to solve our problems on our own. A disciple who still operates within the Tree of Knowledge of Good and Evil cannot fully embrace the calling of God. Instead, a true disciple resides in the Tree of Life, consciously surrendering every aspect of their life to God in each moment.

If our lives do not reflect a genuine commitment to obedience and true discipleship, we must ask ourselves: how can we truly enter into communion with Christ? Can we even call ourselves disciples? Our actions—or lack thereof—may reveal a deeper disbelief in our calling. Without a complete surrender to His will at our conversion, our faith will remain weak, hindering our ability to become effective disciple makers.

Viewing our journey through this lens reveals that true discipleship is rooted in our willingness to wholeheartedly answer His call. As we embrace our identity as followers of Christ, let us strive to bear the fruits of the Spirit (Galatians 5:22-23) that lead us to the Tree of Life, reinforcing our commitment to live in accordance with His teachings and to reflect His love in a world in need of hope.

6. In your walk with God, do you find yourself more focused on worldly problems (Tree of Knowledge of Good and Evil) or on pursuing the Kingdom of God (Tree of Life)? What can you do to refocus your attention on God's Kingdom?

7. Why do you think a disciple who operates from the Tree of Knowledge of Good and Evil cannot fully embrace God's calling?

8. John 17:16 reminds us that we are "not of this world." What does it practically look like for you to live with your allegiance to the Kingdom of God?

9. How do the fruits of the Spirit (Galatians 5:22–23) serve as evidence of someone living from the Tree of Life? Which of these fruits are most and least evident in your life right now?

PRAYER

Lord, help me to fully surrender my life to You. Give me the strength to deny myself, take up my cross, and follow You faithfully. Teach me to embrace the true cost of discipleship and to live for Your Kingdom, not the world. May my heart remain fixed on You as I walk in obedience and trust. In Jesus' name, Amen.

DEEPER THOUGHT AND DISCUSSION

What does it mean to "deny yourself" and "take up your cross" in the context of your daily life? How do these actions reflect the true cost of discipleship? What are some specific areas where God may be calling you to surrender, and how can you take practical steps toward fully committing to Him?

PERSONAL STUDY DAY 3

OVERVIEW:

Many Christians, like Gatungo, hesitate to engage in discipleship due to the influence of religion, which often prioritizes works-based control over developing an authentic relationship with Christ. This creates barriers that hinder our ability to effectively disciple others and fulfill the Great Commission (Matthew 28:19-20). Many Christians don't realize how religious tendencies affect their lives. While they may claim to have a relationship with God, they often exhibit little spiritual fruit and fail to make disciples. Even if they lead successful ministries, the effort often lacks the power of the Holy Spirit.

A closer look reveals that many people try to maintain control over various aspects of their lives. A controlling mindset is at odds with true discipleship, which requires surrender and a willingness to repent. Religious actions like attending church or reading the Bible can become empty rituals when they're done out of obligation rather than genuine obedience to God. These practices often fail to produce true disciples who multiply others.

Mark 7:6–8 (NIV) "These people honor me with their lips, but their hearts are far from me... You have let go of the commands of God and are holding on to human traditions."

PERSONAL APPLICATION:

Key Highlight:

Lifestyles that do not align with God's call to make disciples often operate from a place of religious obligation rather than heartfelt obedience. Such lifestyles fail to produce true fruit and, upon closer examination, are often characterized by worry, anxiety, and fear stemming from the cares of this world. Those who find themselves in this mindset may also judge others and adopt a legalistic attitude, showcasing a superficial understanding of genuine faith.

Dietrich Bonhoeffer characterizes this misguided lifestyle as "cheap grace," a condition marked by legalism that results in significant effort yet yields few, if any, disciples. Learning to identify this dynamic in a disciple's life is crucial for those whose hearts genuinely seek to be surrendered followers of Jesus. It is only through recognizing and addressing these issues that we can cultivate a fruitful and vibrant discipleship experience.

1. What does it mean to approach discipleship with heartfelt obedience instead of obligation? How does this shift affect your motivation and approach?

2. In what ways can you ensure that your efforts in discipleship are not just about checking boxes but about truly helping others grow in their relationship with Jesus?

Key Highlight:

None of us could ever come to Jesus without His grace. As stated in *Ephesians 2:8-9, "For it is by grace you have been saved, through faith—and this is not from yourselves, it is the gift of God—not by works, so that no one can boast."* Religion often pushes us to prove ourselves to others, while our flesh desires to boast. In contrast, God's free gift of grace eliminates this possibility unless one is still trapped in a religious mentality.

A disciple who operates in God's grace can approach the throne room of God with boldness and confidence (Hebrews 4:16), a privilege that a religious person does not have. God's grace equips us with the tools we need to live righteously here on earth. Whenever we face problems or circumstances beyond our control, God's grace is extended to us. This grace is granted when we humble ourselves in God's presence; we must decrease so that He can increase.

As Paul reminds us in *2 Corinthians 12:9, "God said, 'My grace is sufficient for you, for my power is made perfect in weakness.'"* A disciple of God does not try to fix their problems alone; instead, as 1 Peter 5:7 teaches, we cast all our anxiety on Him because He cares for us. Grace enables us to do all of this. If you need peace, God's grace provides it through the Holy Spirit. If you require strength, wisdom, or knowledge, everything is made available to us so that we can bring glory to God.

Many religious individuals believe in these principles but lack the true power that accompanies God's fruit. God's grace calls us to relinquish control and embrace obedience, whereas religion often emphasizes control in our efforts to look good and feel justified.

Operating in God's grace is the only way to have an effective nine-generation discipleship ministry. If religion is your primary source of power, y you will not have a multiplying discipleship ministry.

3. Ephesians 2:8–9 says we are saved by grace, not works. How does this truth challenge the mindset of religious performance or self-justification?

4. According to 2 Corinthians 12:9, God's power is made perfect in our weakness. How does that encourage or challenge you in your current season of life?

5. What are the visible signs of someone operating in God's grace versus someone caught in a religious mindset?

Key Highlight:

We will learn that for a disciple, surrendering to Jesus in our daily lives should be simple: He goes before us, handling the heavy lifting that we once managed on our own, and now we simply follow His lead. Once we gain a clear understanding of what it means to be a disciple and the personal sacrifices this entails, we will find that living a simpler life becomes increasingly apparent as God cultivates a vibrant discipleship ministry through us.

This simpler way of living involves learning to have eyes that see and ears that hear. As we engage with the world around us, we will start to create "God moments" in our conversations, inspired by what we observe Jesus doing in our midst. It is within these transformative encounters that His presence and power are unmistakably revealed in our lives.

A true disciple does not wake up in the morning focused on themselves or how best to serve their own interests. Instead, a disciple rises each day praising and thanking God for another opportunity to serve Him. They have embraced the call to die to themselves and allow God's perspective to shape how they view the world, as described in Luke 9:23.

Disciples are obedient and aware that God is constantly at work around them. They understand that life is not centered on their desires but on glorifying God. With a solid conviction that God is in control of all things, they approach each new day as a precious gift in Christ Jesus.

6. What does it mean for Jesus to "go before us" and handle the heavy lifting in our lives? How does this change the way we approach our daily decisions?

7. What does it mean to have "eyes that see and ears that hear"? How can you become more aware of God at work around you?

8. Luke 9:23 talks about taking up our cross daily. What does that look like practically in your current season of life?

PRAYER

Lord, help me to move beyond mere religious actions and truly surrender to You. Open my heart to obedience, not out of obligation, but out of love for You. Teach me to rely on the Holy Spirit to guide my discipleship and to multiply Your Kingdom through genuine relationships. In Jesus' name, Amen.

DEEPER THOUGHT AND DISCUSSION

- How can we ensure that our discipleship efforts are not merely religious actions done out of obligation, but genuine acts of obedience and surrender?
- What are some practical ways to cultivate a heart of surrender and trust in the Holy Spirit rather than relying on control and legalism?

PERSONAL STUDY DAY 4

OVERVIEW:

The concept of F.A.T. discipleship, which stands for being Faithful, Available, and Teachable—key traits for successful discipleship. A faithful disciple is committed to their calling, obedient, and trustworthy, as seen in scriptures like *Hebrews 10:23 "Let us hold fast the confession of our hope without wavering, for he who promised is faithful."* An available disciple is ready to answer God's call, seeks the good of others, and carries others' burdens, as highlighted in *Isaiah 6:8 "Whom shall I send, and who will go for us?" Then I said, "Here I am! Send me."* Lastly, a teachable disciple is humble, open to learning from anyone, and eager to share what they learn with others, as shown in *Philippians 4:9, "What you have learned and received and heard and seen in me—practice these things, and the God of peace will be with you."* Together, these qualities help build a thriving discipleship ministry.

Exodus 25:9 (NIV) -"Make this tabernacle and all its furnishings exactly like the pattern I will show you."

PERSONAL APPLICATION

Key Highlight:

A faithful person consistently walks in obedience, actively using the gifts they have been given. As *Matthew 25:21 (NIV)* states, *"His master replied, 'Well done, good and faithful servant! You have been faithful with a few things; I will put you in charge of many things. Come and share your master's happiness!"* Lastly, a faithful person is trustworthy. As 1 *Corinthians*

4:2 (NIV) points out, *"Now it is required that those who have been given a trust must prove faithful."*

1. Reflect on areas in your life where you need to remain faithful in your calling and trust God's promises. How can you grow in this stead-fastness?

2. What obstacles might prevent you from being faithful with the gifts you've been given, and how can you overcome them?

3. How can you cultivate a deeper sense of trust and faithfulness in your relationship with God and in your discipleship journey?

Key Highlight:

An available person can be defined as someone who is always ready to respond to God's call when the opportunity arises. This idea is beautifully captured in *Isaiah 6:8 (NIV)*, where the Lord asks, *"Whom shall I send? And who will go for us?"* and the faithful reply comes back, *"Here am I. Send me!"*

Additionally, an available person continually seeks the good of others, as highlighted in *Philippians 2:4 (NIV): "Not looking to your own interests but each of you to the interests of the others."*

Lastly, an available person takes on the burdens of others, thereby fulfilling the law of Christ. *Galatians 6:2 (NIV) states, "Carry each other's burdens, and in this way, you will fulfill the law of Christ."*

An available person is characterized by their readiness to serve, their selflessness, their willingness to adjust their life to God's plans, and their willingness to support those around them.

4. In what ways can we cultivate a heart that is always ready to say, "Here am I. Send me" when God calls us?

5. What are some practical ways you can shift your focus from your own interests to the interests of others?

6. Are there any specific burdens within your community or family that you feel called to help bear?

Key Highlight:

A teachable person is characterized by humility and a willingness to learn from everyone, whether they are new believers or seasoned ministers. Being a disciple of God means being open to lessons from all sources, as beautifully expressed in *Psalm 25:4-5 (NIV): "Show me your ways, Lord, teach me your paths. Guide me in your truth and teach me, for you are God my Savior, and my hope is in you all day long."*

A truly teachable individual never places limits on God; they remain receptive to the idea that He can use anyone—even those outside of the faith—to share wisdom and insights that enrich their lives.

Moreover, a teachable person actively shares the lessons they've learned, creating an environment where God is glorified. *Philippians 4:9 (NIV)* instructs us: *"Whatever you have learned or received or heard from me or seen in me—put it into practice. And the God of peace will be with you."*

A teachable individual approaches life with an open heart and mind, eager to learn, share, and grow in faith no matter whom God uses to speak into their lives.

7. How does Psalm 25:4-5 influence your perspective on being teachable?

8. How can we recognize when God is using someone or something unexpected to open our eyes to what He is doing?

9. What are some examples from your life where you've put into practice the lessons you've received, as mentioned in Philippians 4:9?

10. What are some practical steps you can take to remain teachable in your relationship with God and others?

PRAYER

Lord, thank You for calling me to be faithful, available, and teachable. Help me to renew my mind and transform my heart to reflect Your will. Guide me to walk in obedience, ready to serve, and open to learn from You and others. Empower me to live out these qualities in my discipleship journey and to make a lasting impact for Your Kingdom. In Jesus' name, Amen.

DEEPER THOUGHT AND DISCUSSION

Being Faithful, Available, and Teachable requires a transformed heart, not just outward actions. As *Romans 12:2 (NIV)* says, *"Do not conform to the pattern of this world, but be transformed by the renewing of your mind."* This transformation empowers us to live out these traits in our discipleship journey.

- How does Romans 12:2 challenge you in your walk as a faithful, available, and teachable disciple?
- What worldly patterns might hinder you from living out these qualities?
- How can the renewal of your mind through the Holy Spirit help you follow God's will more fully?

PERSONAL STUDY DAY 5

OVERVIEW:

The importance of setting a high standard in discipleship is to draw inspiration from Jesus' example. Jesus called His followers to be wholly committed, not part-time, urging them to leave behind their past lives for a radical, single-minded devotion to Him. Discipleship requires total surrender to Christ, trusting that He will supply all our needs. The section highlights that to build a thriving discipleship ministry, we must set high expectations for ourselves and others, focusing on disciples who are Faithful, Available, and Teachable (F.A.T.). Additionally, the section underscores the significance of building a strong leadership team, as Jesus did, selecting those ready to follow Him. A solid leadership team amplifies ministry impact and fosters a spiritual movement, extending God's work across the globe. The ultimate goal is to create a ministry that spreads the message of Christ and transforms lives through the power of effective discipleship.

1 Corinthians 9:24–27 (NIV) - "Run in such a way as to get the prize... I discipline my body like an athlete..."

PERSONAL APPLICATION

Key Highlight:

A thriving discipleship ministry is to follow Jesus' example in setting a high standard for His disciples. He established an unwavering benchmark, clearly indicating that He sought followers who were committed wholeheartedly, not just part-time. Jesus challenged them to embrace a radical lifestyle, urging them to leave behind their nets and everything that defined their past (Matthew 4:19-20). There was never any suggestion from Jesus that they could straddle two worlds; His call required total devotion and singular focus.

Setting a high bar in discipleship is essential as we work to cultivate a culture of multiplication—where disciples not only grow in their relationship with Christ but are also empowered to make more disciples themselves. Paul's words in *2 Timothy 2:2* remind us of this calling: *"And the things you have heard me say in the presence of many witnesses entrust to reliable people who will also be qualified to teach others."* This process of raising the bar encourages accountability, growth, and a deeper commitment to the mission of Christ.

1. What does it mean to follow Jesus' example of wholehearted commitment rather than a part-time approach?

2. What does it mean to "leave behind our nets" in the context of our current lives? What are some things we need to let go of to fully follow Jesus?

3. Why is it important to set a high bar in discipleship, especially in a culture that often values comfort and convenience?

Key Highlight:

It is important to note that Jesus did not disciple everyone; He focused on those whom God revealed to Him as being ready to follow and learn. This selective approach teaches us that in building a thriving discipleship leadership team, we, too, must be discerning about whom we invest our time and energy in. Meeting for coffee to disciple someone will take on a deeper significance as we embrace Jesus' style of discipleship.

Building a solid leadership team is not just beneficial; it is critical. Jesus demonstrated the incredible power of teamwork among His disciples, showcasing how collaboration and mutual support can amplify ministry impact.

In *Matthew 18:20*, Jesus assures us, *"For where two or three gather in my name, there am I with them."* This verse reinforces the importance of gathering in fellowship and intentionality. By following Jesus' model, we will learn how to cultivate a leadership team that reflects His values and commitment, turning our ministries into powerful movements that can change lives and transform communities.

4. In what ways can we embrace a more intentional and focused approach to discipleship, similar to Jesus' style?

5. What impact can a deep, personal discipleship relationship have on both the individual being discipled and the person doing the discipling?

6. What are the key elements that make a leadership team in discipleship effective and solid?

Key Highlights:

We will learn that ultimately, these principles will shape our vision for achieving the ultimate goal of discipleship: to have a powerful ministry used by God, where a spiritual movement takes place that transcends boundaries and spreads the message of Christ throughout the world. *Matthew 9:37-38*, where Jesus says, *"The harvest is plentiful, but the workers are few. Ask the Lord of the harvest, therefore, to send out workers into his harvest field."* Together, we can become those workers, ready to embrace the call of discipleship and transform lives.

Every disciple should envision fostering a spiritual movement within their personal discipleship ministry. Across the globe, countless individuals are applying these principles and sharing testimonies of the extraordinary work God is doing; work that has transcended their immediate influence. They are hearing stories of those they have discipled, who in turn are becoming empowered to create their own movements of God. The reach of God's work in these ministries has expanded to levels that are truly beyond tracking.

7. What does it mean to be a "worker" in God's harvest field? How are you currently serving in this role—or how might God be calling you to step into it?

8. What does a spiritual movement look like to you? Can you envision one starting within your personal discipleship efforts?

9. What fears or limitations might prevent you from believing that God can use your ministry to spark a spiritual movement?

PRAYER

Thank You for the radical example of discipleship that Jesus set before us. Help me to embrace the call to follow Him with wholehearted commitment, leaving behind what holds me back and fully surrendering to Your will. Give me wisdom and discernment as I invest in others and build a strong, multiplying discipleship ministry. May I always strive to set high standards, just as Jesus did, and trust You to equip and empower me to walk this path faithfully. In Jesus' name, Amen.

DEEPER THOUGHT AND DISCUSSION:

Jesus didn't just call His followers to be committed, but to engage in a radical transformation that changes their entire identity. He cast vision and showed His disciples the importance of reaching the whole world in His name. In the same way, we should follow His example by casting vision with those we disciple. Let them know that they, too, are called to make disciples—who will make more disciples. Help them see that, over time, their personal ministry can multiply into thousands of lives transformed by Jesus, spreading across neighborhoods, nations, and generations.

He required them to step away from their past attachments and embrace a new purpose in Him. This call isn't just about what we do; it's about who we are becoming in Christ.

Session 1 Casting Clear Vision - Song

Song Title: Walking in His Vision

There comes a moment in every disciple's journey when we stop chasing our own plans and begin walking in the vision Jesus has for us. This song is a declaration of surrender—stepping out of the ordinary and into God's purpose.

As we walk in His vision, we're also called to cast vision for those we lead—helping them discover their own calling in Christ.

Bible Verse:

"I will instruct you and teach you in the way you should go; I will counsel you with my loving eye on you." -Psalm 32:8 (NIV)

♫ ♫ **Scan the QR code to listen and be reminded: your steps—and theirs—have eternal purpose.**

https://youtu.be/_cbaAGrf2
E8

Chapter 2

Session 2 Define Your Mission (purpose)

To get the most out of your daily personal study, begin by reading the corresponding chapter from the book. This provides the context you will need to reflect deeply and answer the questions thoughtfully. While the study guide focuses on the first eight chapters—each divided into five sections for daily reflection—the book also includes four additional training chapters to further equip you.

Start each day in prayer, inviting the Holy Spirit to open your heart and show you what He wants you to see. As you work through the questions, do so with honesty, vulnerability, and humility. Let the Holy Spirit lead you, shape you, and bring lasting transformation through this journey.

PERSONAL STUDY DAY 1

OVERVIEW:

This session explores how people often define their purpose and contrasts common cultural views with a biblical perspective. Many individuals, including Christians, tend to describe their purpose in terms of personal ambition, career goals, or family roles. For example, one Christian woman expressed her purpose as creating her own opportunities and forging her path through determination and effort—a mindset that reflects a self-focused and success-driven approach influenced by the world.

In contrast, Scripture offers a different view of purpose—one centered on humility, service to others, and alignment with God's will. Verses like Proverbs 9:10, Matthew 13:16, and John 10:27 highlight that true wisdom begins with a reverent relationship with God, and that our purpose is discovered by seeing life through His perspective and listening to His voice. Instead of striving for self-promotion, we are called to live in a close relationship with God and reflect His character in our actions. While statements like "I want to glorify God in all I do" are well-intentioned, it's important to explore what that actually looks like in everyday life through specific, God-honoring choices and relationships.

Romans 12:1-2 (NIV) "Therefore, I urge you, brothers and sisters... to offer your bodies as a living sacrifice... Do not conform to the pattern of this world but be transformed by the renewing of your mind."

PERSONAL APPLICATION

Key Highlight:

Failing to see the world through Jesus' eyes can lead us to a life purpose centered on self-promotion, dedication, and hard work—an inward focus. In contrast, cultivating an intimate relationship with God and serving others aligns our purpose with His desires for our lives.

1. What does it mean to "see the world through Jesus' eyes"?

2. Can you identify areas in your life where your purpose has been more inwardly focused (e.g., on success, recognition, or achievement)?

3. Read John 10:27 and Proverbs 9:10. What do these verses teach about hearing God's voice and gaining wisdom?

<u>Key Highlight:</u>

God's grace is the foundation of discipleship; through God's unmerited favor and love, we are enabled to follow Jesus and live as His disciples. When we enter into this grace, we accept that things are now different and that our lives are no longer about ourselves; instead, they are about God and serving Him in fulfilling His desires for our lives. So why do so many Christians struggle with this fact? As Paul shares in *1 Corinthians 6:20, "You were bought at a price; therefore, honor God with your bodies."* This emphasizes that it is no longer ourselves that are living, but rather Christ who now lives within us (Galatians 2:20).

4. How would you define God's grace in your own words?

5. In what ways is life "no longer about ourselves" once we become followers of Jesus?

6. Why do you think many Christians struggle with fully embracing a life that is about God rather than themselves?

Key Highlight:

When we surrender our lives to God, we are essentially giving up control and choosing to follow His purposes, directions, and commandments for our lives. By relinquishing our personal rights, in surrender to God's grace we gain the rewards and benefits of a new life in Christ. At first, we may struggle to fully comprehend how this new life in Christ will transform us. Our old habits and ways of living linger, leading to confusion for many Christians regarding their true purpose. This clash between the old and new can create uncertainty as we seek to understand what it means to live in alignment with God's calling.

7. What are some personal "rights" or areas of control that are difficult for you to let go of?

8. How have you experienced transformation—or resistance to transformation—since choosing to follow Jesus?

9. Why do old habits and ways of thinking often linger even after we've committed our lives to Christ?

> **PRAYER**
>
> Father, Thank You for Your grace that gives me a new life in Christ. I want to surrender fully to You—my plans, my desires, and my need for control. Help me let go and trust Your purpose for my life. When I struggle with old habits or feel confused about what You're calling me to, remind me that I belong to You. Help me see through Jesus' eyes, hear His voice, and walk closely with You each day.
>
> In Jesus' name, Amen.

DEEPER THOUGHT AND DISCUSSION

At the heart of the Christian life is a radical shift—from living for ourselves to living for God. This transformation is not based on our effort but on God's grace, which invites us into a new identity and purpose. Yet, this journey is not without tension. We often wrestle with old habits, lingering self-focus, and the cultural pressure to define success through personal achievement.

Surrendering to God doesn't mean we become passive—it means we actively trust Him with our direction and identity. It's choosing to align our daily lives with His desires, not just with big decisions, but in the small, unseen acts of obedience, humility, and service.

The struggle lies in the overlap of the old and new—we may know we've been made new in Christ, but it can feel like we're still living in two worlds: one that chases personal greatness, and one that calls us to Christlike surrender.

So, the question becomes: Are we building our lives around who we want to become, or around who God is calling us to be?

PERSONAL STUDY DAY 2

OVERVIEW:

Over time, with obedience, old habits will fade, replaced by new habits, and understanding God's grace gives us eyes to see His truth more clearly. This journey is not a sprint but a marathon, requiring patience as you unlearn old ways and embrace God's new ones (Colossians 3:10).

2 Timothy 1:9 (NIV)

"He has saved us and called us to a holy life—not because of anything we have done but because of his own purpose and grace..."

PERSONAL APPLICATION:

Key Highlight:

In *1 Corinthians 9:24-27* (ESV), Paul writes: *"Do you not know that in a race all the runners run, but only one receives the prize? So run that you may obtain it. Every athlete exercises self-control in all things. They do it to receive a perishable wreath, but we an imperishable. So, I do not run aimlessly; I do not box as one beating the air. But I discipline my body and keep it under control, lest after preaching to others I myself should be disqualified."*

To overcome our old habits, we must cultivate new ones according to Gods word, which requires a disciplined lifestyle. Picture your newfound life purpose as a daily commitment—an ongoing duty to report for action each day.

1. What does Paul mean when he compares the Christian life to a race?

2. In what areas of your life do you struggle with self-control? How can you apply discipline to these areas in light of God's word?

3. What new habits do you feel God is calling you to cultivate in order to live according to His word?

<u>Key Highlight:</u>

Begin each morning by defining your mission by praising God and reaffirming your commitment to Him. Acknowledge His sovereignty and express gratitude for His mercy and grace, as described in *Lamentations 3:22-23: "Because of the Lord's great love we are not consumed, for his compassions never fail. They are new every morning; great is your faithfulness."*

Set aside your personal desires to seek His will for your life, ensuring your alignment with His character through time spent in His Word (Psalm 119:105). Not merely as a ritualistic habit devoid of change, but as a heartfelt devotion of surrender that consistently leads to obedience. In doing so, you will allow His love to shape you, embracing who you are as He made you while finding contentment in the gifts He has given (Ephesians 2:10).

4. How does starting your day with gratitude and worship affect your mindset and actions?

5. How can you practice daily surrender in a way that feels genuine rather than just routine?

6. Psalm 119:105 describes God's Word as a lamp and light. How has Scripture guided you in your personal decisions and spiritual growth?

Key Highlight:

Understand that you are a small yet significant part of His grand plan. However, God cannot share His mission with you if you do not make Him your number one priority. Each day, He has a 'mission report' for you, delivered during your time of prayer and reading His Word. Through His guidance and your obedience, you begin to fulfill what He has laid out for you each day (Jeremiah 29:11).

In His presence, you are continually humbled, He is glorified, and you gain the ability to see and love the world through His eyes. This daily practice of surrender requires discipline, but it also aligns you with His purpose, preparing you to fulfill your role in being and making disciples.

Remember, this journey with Christ requires perseverance and dedication.

7. What does it mean to you to be a "small yet significant" part of God's grand plan?

8. Why is it essential to make God your number one priority if you want to understand His mission for your life?

9. How does aligning with God's purpose prepare you to be and make disciples?

> ### *PRAYER*
>
> Father, Thank You for choosing me to be part of Your greater plan. Help me to make You my first priority each day, to hear Your voice through prayer and Your Word, and to walk in obedience to what You reveal. Teach me to see the world through Your eyes, to love as You love, and to fulfill the purpose You've set before me. Strengthen me to surrender daily, and give me the perseverance to follow You with faith and joy. In Jesus' name, Amen.

DEEPER THOUGHT AND DISCUSSION

As followers of Christ, we're not just invited into salvation—we're called into a mission. But that mission isn't something we stumble upon accidentally. It flows from a life of daily connection with God, where He is the priority, not a side note.

God desires to share His heart with us, but if we're too distracted, too rushed, or too focused on ourselves, we miss it. His "mission report" is delivered daily—in the quiet moments of prayer and the truth of His Word. Through surrender and obedience, we begin to live not just for God, but with Him.

The challenge? It's not just one act of surrender. It's a continual choice—a disciplined lifestyle of dying to self, seeking His will, and loving others with His eyes. This is how we step into our role in God's story. And though the journey is long and sometimes difficult, He walks with us, giving grace for each step and strength to persevere.

PERSONAL STUDY DAY 3

OVERVIEW:

A mission is often described as a clear and specific purpose or goal that directs actions and decisions. It typically involves a broader, long-term objective that guides individuals or organizations.

On a personal level, a mission refers to one's core purpose or calling in life. It is what motivates and gives meaning to one's actions. For instance, someone might feel their mission is to support others through counseling or to advance scientific research. In a business context, a mission statement outlines the company's primary purpose, goals, and values, guiding decision-making and strategy. For example, a non-profit may have a mission to eradicate poverty, while a business might focus on providing innovative technology solutions. In the military, a mission refers to a specific assignment or operation with strategic objectives.

Overall, a mission provides a clear, purposeful direction that steers actions and decisions towards achieving specific goals or fulfilling a higher calling.

Colossians 3:23-24 (NIV) - "Whatever you do, work at it with all your heart, as working for the Lord, not for human masters..."

PERSONAL APPLICATION:

Key Highlight:

As disciples of Christ, we also have our own mission, which involves our divine purpose and calling. Every day, we receive a new mission report from God. He shares His desires for our life and instructs us to live it out loud and share what He has taught us with our friends. He wants us to be the person He created us to be. His desire is for us to align our life with His plans, rather than choosing our own path. As a disciple, we must reflect the characteristics of a disciple and not something else.

1. What does it mean to you to have a personal mission as a disciple of Christ?

2. What gifts or qualities has God placed in you that can be used for His mission?

3. How comfortable are you sharing what God is teaching you with friends or others around you?

4. What holds you back from living your faith "out loud," and how can you overcome that?

Key Highlight:

My friend and colleague Geoffrey once illustrated this with an analogy: if an assembly line is intended to produce mobile phones but ends up producing something else, the company is clearly not in the mobile phone business. Similarly, if we identify as disciples of Jesus but are not actively making other disciples, we are missing our true mission and purpose.

5. How does this illustration help clarify the true purpose of a disciple?

6. If someone looked at the "output" of your life, would it reflect the mission of making disciples? Why or why not?

7. Just like an assembly line can be realigned to produce the right product, how can we realign ourselves to return to the mission of making disciples?

Key Highlight:

There is nothing in life worth pursuing without God's anointing in our lives. We are continually learning and growing in the Lord, and we will not fully arrive until we are in heaven. Operating our ministry without God's anointing will yield no fruit, both in our ministry efforts and in the disciples, we seek to cultivate.

To grasp how to make multiplying disciples, we must first challenge ourselves daily with the question: Are we anointed by God to fulfill the mission He has set before us?

8. Why is it dangerous or ineffective to pursue ministry or disciple-making without God's anointing?

9. What does it look like to ask yourself daily: "Am I anointed by God to fulfill this mission?

> **PRAYER**
>
> Lord, I don't want to walk in my own strength or miss the mission You've placed before me. Anoint me for the work You've called me to. Keep me humble, growing, and dependent on You. Help me to bear fruit that lasts by making disciples who follow You deeply. Align my heart with Yours and may everything I do bring glory to Your name. In Jesus' name, Amen.

DEEPER THOUGHT AND DISCUSSION

Many people step into ministry or spiritual leadership with good intentions, but not every effort is anointed by God. There's a big difference between working for God and working with God—between striving in our own strength and being led by the Spirit. Without God's anointing, even our best efforts will fall flat and bear no eternal fruit.

Discipleship isn't just about doing more—it's about becoming more like Christ and helping others do the same. And that starts with daily surrender, dependence on God's power, and a willingness to ask: Am I walking in God's calling, or just my own plans?

We also have to remember that making disciples isn't a one-time event—it's a lifestyle of multiplication, empowered by God's presence. If we're not connected to Him, we're like branches cut off from the vine (John 15:5)—unable to bear fruit, no matter how busy we are.

PERSONAL STUDY DAY 4

OVERVIEW:

Ephesians 2:10 (NIV) - "For we are God's handiwork, created in Christ Jesus to do good works, which God prepared in advance for us to do."

PERSONAL APPLICATION

Key Highlight:

When I first began to ask myself these challenging questions, I struggled to understand my own mission. Despite being active in church—attending services, leading Bible study groups, and going on mission trips—I did not fully grasp God's calling or purpose for my life.

While I professed my commitment to God's work, I found myself more preoccupied with financial gain and often living in sin. Honestly, I cannot say that I had the anointing of God upon my life; there was little fruit being produced, and disciple-making was not taking place.

In the past, if someone were to ask me about my purpose, I would have answered that it was to live for God and make a difference in the world around me. While I often spoke about these ideals and presented myself as if I were walking closely with God, deep down, I still struggled to grasp the essence of my true purpose.

1. The writer admits to living in sin and being preoccupied with financial gain while appearing committed to God's work. Can you relate to seasons where your actions didn't fully match your intentions or beliefs? Share an example.

2. What does it look like when there's little spiritual fruit in someone's life, despite a lot of activity?

3. What steps can we take to move from confusion about our purpose into clarity and alignment with God's calling?

Key Highlight:

God posed two profound questions: "How can you claim to be My disciple if you do not love others as I do?" and "How can you be My disciple if you do not follow My teachings and trust Me completely with your life?"

These questions humbled me deeply, it was as if for the first time in my life, I was able to hear God speak to me. In His mercy, God led me to *Galatians 5:16-26*, which speaks to the heart of discipleship.

"But I say, walk by the Spirit, and you will not gratify the desires of the flesh. For the desires of the flesh are against the Spirit, and the desires of the Spirit are against the flesh, for these are opposed to each other, to keep you from doing the things you want to do. But if you are led by the Spirit, you are not under the law.

Now the works of the flesh are evident: sexual immorality, impurity, sensuality, idolatry, sorcery, enmity, strife, jealousy, fits of anger, rivalries, dissensions, divisions, envy, drunkenness, orgies, and things like these. I warn you, as I warned you before, that those who do such things will not inherit the kingdom of God.

But the fruit of the Spirit is love, joy, peace, patience, kindness, goodness, faithfulness, gentleness, self-control; against such things there is no law. And those who belong to Christ Jesus have crucified the flesh with its passions and desires. If we live by the Spirit, let us also keep in step with the Spirit. Let us not become conceited, provoking one another, envying one another."

4. What do God's questions "How can you claim to be My disciple if you do not love others as I do?" and "How can you be My disciple if you do not follow My teachings and trust Me completely?"—stir in your heart?

5. Have you ever had a moment where you felt God speak to you so clearly it shifted your perspective? What was that like?

6. According to this passage, what does it mean to walk by the Spirit, and how does that contrast with living by the flesh?

<u>Key Highlight:</u>

God reset my purpose and revealed that intimacy with Him is what matters most. Jesus commands us to *"Love the Lord your God with all your heart, with all your soul, and with all your mind" (Matthew 22:37)*, and to *"Love your neighbor as yourself" (Matthew 22:39)*. My journey began with learning to empty myself and understanding that everything in life begins and ends with Him. As Paul writes, *"For in Him we live and move and have our being" (Acts 17:28)*. Knowing Him and being known by Him is of utmost importance.

Once I felt I was on solid ground, God revealed a major reason for my spiritual stagnation: I was not discipling others. I lacked an outlet to share the incredible things God was teaching me. This realization marked the beginning of understanding my mission. I came to see that the command to "Go and make disciples of all nations" (Matthew 28:19) was not merely a suggestion but a divine command. This understanding unlocked what was previously closed and ignited a spiritual revival within me. Discipling others became my passion, and in these moments, God spoke to me profoundly.

7. How do you create space in your life to be known by God—not just to serve Him, but to truly connect with Him?

8. Have you ever considered that not discipling others could lead to spiritual stagnation? Why do you think that happens?

9. What barriers might be keeping you from actively making disciples? How can you begin to overcome them?

> **PRAYER**
>
> Lord, thank You for calling me into a deeper relationship with You. Help me to love You with all my heart, soul, and mind, and to love others as You do. Teach me to walk closely with You, to find my purpose in knowing You, and to respond to Your command to make disciples. Awaken my heart to the mission You've given me, and let Your Spirit guide me in every step. In Jesus' name, Amen.

DEEPER THOUGHT AND DISCUSSION

Many believers desire a close relationship with God but unknowingly miss a vital part of that intimacy—obedience to the call to make disciples. True intimacy with God isn't just about personal devotion; it's also about spiritual reproduction. Jesus didn't just call us to know Him; He commanded us to go in His name.

When we hold back from sharing what God is doing in us, we limit the growth He wants to do through us. Often, we feel spiritually stagnant not because we aren't receiving enough—but because we aren't pouring out what we've already been given.

Discipleship is the overflow of intimacy with Christ. It's in walking closely with Him that we're empowered to walk with others. And it's often in discipling others that our understanding of God becomes more real, more tested, and more alive.

PERSONAL STUDY DAY 5

OVERVIEW:

Paul often employs military imagery to illustrate the Christian mission. In *2 Timothy 2:3-4 (NIV), he encourages Timothy to endure hardship as a "good soldier of Christ Jesus,"* stressing that a soldier focuses on pleasing their commanding officer rather than getting distracted by civilian affairs. A disciple of Jesus is anointed by God to fulfill His purposes for His glory, fully surrendered and adopting a soldier's mentality to complete their mission. This means walking away from their own preconceived notions of life's mission and embracing what God defines as their true purpose.

Philippians 1:21 (NIV) - "For to me, to live is Christ and to die is gain."

PERSONAL APPLICATION

Key Highlight:

James 1:22 states, "Do not merely listen to the word, and so deceive yourselves. Do what it says." This verse beautifully illustrates the distinction between religion and relationship. Religious individuals may have knowledge of God's Word, believe it comes from Him, attend church, and partake in religious duties. In contrast, those who have a genuine relationship with God engage in all the same activities as religious people, but they actively read His Word, meditate on it, and strive to be obedient.

1. Why do you think James warns us about deceiving ourselves by only listening to the Word?

2. How would you personally define the difference between being religious and having a relationship with God?

3. Is there a recent area of your life where God has called you to act on His Word? What happened when you responded—or didn't?

Key Highlight:

Obedience to God's Word not only grants us freedom and power but, more importantly, fosters a deeper connection with Him, allowing us to enter His presence daily to hear His voice. These are crucial questions that require honest introspection. The key to understanding your mission and purpose lies in your daily transformation time with Jesus. Prioritizing being broken in His presence each day is essential; otherwise, you will struggle to fulfill your mission and align with God's purpose for your life.

4. How have you seen obedience to God's Word bring freedom or power in your own life?

5. The phrase "being broken in His presence" is powerful. What does that mean to you personally?

6. How would your life look different if you consistently aligned each day with God's purpose?

Key Highlight:

Are you on the assembly line producing disciples in how you were created to produce (Relationship), or are you producing something entirely different (Religion)? A true disciple understands their mission is to produce other God-fearing disciples who, in turn, make more God-fearing disciples.

If you had asked me these questions years ago, I would have said that while I had a desire to produce disciples, I was not fulfilling God's calling of making disciples the way I should be. I would have recognized that I had a long way to go, which would have motivated me to seek out more opportunities for learning and growth.

7. How can you tell the difference between religious activity and relational disciple-making?

8. What has helped—or hindered—you in becoming more intentional about making disciples?

9. Who in your life could you begin to invest in spiritually as part of living out your mission?

PRAYER

Lord, thank You for calling me into a relationship with You—not just religion, but real, daily intimacy. Help me walk in obedience, seek Your presence each day, and stay aligned with the mission You've given me. Teach me to produce disciples who know and love You deeply. Keep my heart humble, my spirit willing, and my purpose clear. In Jesus' name, Amen.

DEEPER THOUGHT AND DISCUSSION:

Many believers live as though checking off religious boxes—attending church, reading Scripture, or volunteering—equates to spiritual maturity. But Jesus never called us to religion. He called us into deep relationship with Him that transforms us and leads us to reproduce that transformation in others.

A true disciple doesn't just consume spiritual content—they live it out in obedience and help others grow in their walk with Christ. Jesus didn't say, "Admire Me," He said, "Follow Me." The difference is seen in what we produce with our lives. Are we simply maintaining our faith, or are we multiplying it?

Imagine your life as an assembly line: are you producing what God designed you to produce—spirit-filled disciples—or something else entirely? That question cuts to the heart of our mission.

Session 2 - Define your mission (Purpose) - Song

Song Title: Surrendered Eyes

Surrendered Eyes is a call to obedience—to follow Jesus with vision fully aligned to His mission. When our eyes are surrendered, we no longer chase what's temporary. We focus on what matters most: making disciples and living for eternity.

This kind of vision requires daily surrender. As we follow Jesus, we must train those we lead to fix their eyes on Him—and walk in bold obedience to His call.

Bible Verse:

"Let us run with endurance the race that is set before us, fixing our eyes on Jesus, the pioneer and perfecter of faith." —Hebrews 12:1b–2a (NIV)

♫ ♫ **Scan the QR code to listen and renew your focus: surrendered eyes lead to obedient lives**

https://youtu.be/
itsxU_G4GLo

Chapter 3

Session 3 Eyes to See

To get the most out of your daily personal study, begin by reading the corresponding chapter from the book. This provides the context you will need to reflect deeply and answer the questions thoughtfully. While the study guide focuses on the first eight chapters—each divided into five sections for daily reflection—the book also includes four additional training chapters to further equip you.

Start each day in prayer, inviting the Holy Spirit to open your heart and show you what He wants you to see. As you work through the questions, do so with honesty, vulnerability, and humility. Let the Holy Spirit lead you, shape you, and bring lasting transformation through this journey.

Personal Study Day 1

OVERVIEW:

The goal of this session is to guide disciples in learning to perceive their lives through God's eyes, while also addressing the reasons they may not currently be doing so. Our lives should operate at the pace of God in contentment, but that can only happen if we can see life through His eyes.

In *Matthew 13:9*, Jesus emphasizes, *"Anyone with ears to hear should listen and understand."* Here, He conveys to His disciples that without drawing near to Him, true understanding of His words is elusive. The disciples had yet to learn how to perceive circumstances or parables through God's eyes; they consistently struggled to grasp the spiritual dimensions of their experiences.

1 Corinthians 2:14 (ESV) – "The natural person does not accept the things of the Spirit of God, for they are folly to him... because they are spiritually discerned."

PERSONAL APPLICATION

Key Highlight:

In an effort to help His disciples, Jesus employed parables. However, even then, they questioned His method. In *Mathew 13:10*, they asked, *"Why do you use parables when you talk to the people?"* Jesus replied in verse 11, *"You are permitted to understand the secrets of the Kingdom of Heaven, but others are not."* This distinction illustrates that those who do not follow God are unable to comprehend spiritual truths. Consequently, when faced with life's challenges or parables that mirror them, they struggle to find meaning or guidance, often resorting to responses shaped by their cultural norms and habitual behaviors.

Jesus exhibits patience with His disciples. In verse 12, He clarifies why many are left in confusion: *"To those who listen to my teaching, more understanding will be given, and they will have an abundance of knowledge. But for those who are not listening, even what little understanding they have will be taken away from them."* Essentially, the closer we draw near to Jesus, the clearer our vision becomes regarding life's circumstances; conversely, distancing ourselves from Him leads to confusion and bewilderment.

In verse 13, Jesus elaborates, stating, *"This is why I use these parables: for they look, but they don't really see. They hear, but they don't truly listen or understand."* This notion is not novel;

it echoes the prophetic message given to Isaiah in *Isaiah 6:9-10: "When you hear what I say, you will not understand. When you see what I do, you will not comprehend."*

1. In Matthew 13:11, Jesus makes a distinction between those who are permitted to understand and those who are not. How does that challenge or encourage you in your own walk with God?

2. According to Jesus, what separates someone who "hears" from someone who truly listens and understands?

3. What are some modern-day "cultural norms" or habits that might cloud our spiritual vision, like Jesus described in verse 13?

Key Highlight:

The followers of God possess a supernatural ability to discern spiritual truths; those who do not belong to Him cannot access this understanding. Recognizing that God controls the overarching narrative of life allows us to trust in Him rather than being overwhelmed by the cares of this world.

Despite their questions, the disciples sought more clarity. In *Mathew 13:15*, Jesus explains that the issue lies in the hardness of people's hearts: He said, *"Their ears cannot hear, and they have closed their eyes—so their eyes cannot see, and their ears cannot hear, and their hearts cannot understand; they cannot turn to me and let me heal them."*

4. What do you think it means to have a "supernatural ability" to discern spiritual truths? Have you ever experienced that kind of clarity in your walk with God?

5. Who in your life models the kind of spiritual discernment and trust described in this passage? What do you notice about how they live?

6. Jesus describes people whose hearts have grown hard, and whose eyes and ears are closed. What might cause someone's heart to become that way—slow to hear or understand God's truth?

7. Are there any areas of your life right now where you're seeking clarity from God? How are you positioning yourself to hear His voice?

Key Highlight:

When God looks at people, He sees lost sheep in need of a shepherd. Rather than condemning or belittling them, He speaks words of life and longs for a loving relationship with each one of us. As we respond in obedience and embrace His truth as active doers of His Word, our eyes are opened to see others through His perspective.

If our habits are shaped by the things of this world, our hearts can grow hardened, blinding us to God's view. When a disciple's focus is on self-fulfillment, it becomes increasingly difficult to perceive others as God does. This self-centeredness hampers our ability to hear and respond to His daily call.

8. How does it change your view of others to know that God sees them as "lost sheep" rather than problems or enemies?

9. What does it mean to speak words of life to those around us? What might that look like in your everyday conversations?

10. What are some warning signs that our hearts might be growing hard or blind to God's view of others?

11. What is one step you can take this week to see someone the way God sees them—and to respond with compassion and intentionality?

PRAYER

Lord, Thank You for inviting me into deeper relationship and understanding with You. Soften my heart and remove anything that blinds me to Your truth. Give me eyes to see and ears to hear, that I may recognize Your voice, receive Your wisdom, and respond with obedience.

Help me to see people the way You see them—with compassion, grace, and purpose. Teach me to walk in love, not judgment, and to speak words of life that reflect Your heart. Keep me from being shaped by the world, and instead, shape me daily by Your Spirit. May I stay close to You and live as a faithful doer of Your Word.

In Jesus' name, Amen.

DEEPER THOUGHT AND DISCUSSION

When we drift from Jesus—becoming self-focused and tuning in to the noise of the world—we begin to form hardened habits that cloud our vision and dull our spiritual senses. But the more we lean into Him—not just to hear His words, but to live them—the more clearly, we begin to see the world, and people, through His eyes.

Jesus didn't just want His disciples to "understand" with their minds—He wanted them to be transformed in how they live, love, and see.

In *Matthew 13*, He is essentially saying: *"If you really want to understand, come close. Keep listening. Keep following. I will help you see."*

Personal Study Day 2

OVERVIEW:

Peter, Andrew, James, and John were fishermen by trade, spending their days catching fish to pay their bills and build wealth. It is likely that their conversations centered around their work, surrounding themselves with others who shared their worldview. Their profession not only shaped their culture but also established habits that influenced their decision-making. When Jesus called them, He understood this deeply and met them where they were. He recognized that they viewed people through a transactional lens, seeing others as either allies who could help them achieve their ambitions or adversaries who stood in their way.

Not only were they fishermen by trade, but they were also good Jewish boys who regularly attended synagogue and participated in their cultural and religious duties. Their attendance was a part of their upbringing, a tradition they observed because it was expected. They learned about Yahweh and believed in the teachings they heard during their time of worship. They faithfully engaged in Jewish rituals such as Passover, Shabbat, circumcision, and Yom Kippur, fulfilling their religious obligations. To those around them, they appeared to be model Jews, diligently checking off all the boxes of their faith and leading lives that aligned with societal expectations.

Yet despite fulfilling these external religious duties, their worldview often limited their understanding of God's greater purpose.

Hosea 6:6 "I want you to show love, not offer sacrifices. I want you to know me more than I want burnt offerings."

PERSONAL APPLICATION:

<u>Key Highlight:</u>

The disciples viewed their mission through the lens of personal gain, unaware that their true calling lay in recognizing the intrinsic value of every individual. The Bible is filled with stories of how the disciples sought to take control when situations did not align with their narrative. One striking example is Peter in John 18:10, who cut off the ear of Malchus, the high priest's servant, because he believed this was the right course of action. In that moment, Peter failed to see Malchus through God's eyes, viewing him instead only through the lens of personal gain and self-interest.

Peter reacted instinctively, shaped by a culture that reinforced the notion that such a response was normal when things did not go his way. His habitual reactions were deeply ingrained, but it would take a profound encounter with Jesus to challenge this perspective. That encounter would invite him into a transformative relationship, elevating his understanding of purpose and community

1. How does viewing our mission through the lens of personal gain distort the way we see others and our calling?

2. What does Peter's reaction in John 18:10 reveal about his mindset and expectations of how God's plan should unfold?

3. What helps you move from reaction-based living to Spirit-led response? What practices can help you respond with God's heart instead of your own?

Key Highlight:

At its core, religion is typically defined as a structured system of beliefs, practices, and values that often centers around questions of existence, morality, and the divine. It provides individuals with a sense of purpose and a mission, influencing culture, law, and personal behavior. Through religion, people find a framework for understanding the world and their place within it.

Belief systems can take many forms; we may worship our own self-interest, as Peter did, creating personal cultural ecosystems rooted in our own beliefs and desires. It is also possible to blend personal beliefs with organized religion, seeking some kind of balance in our understanding of our lives. Religion helps us stay focused on our goals, and when faced with opposition to our belief system, we often react defensively, disregarding those who challenge our views. Our understanding of the world is filtered through our beliefs, leading us to assess relationships based on similarity to our own values and ideals, categorizing people as allies or outsiders.

4. How would you define the difference between religion and a personal relationship with God? Can they coexist in a healthy way?

5. How can we engage with those who challenge or disagree with our beliefs in a way that reflects Jesus instead of reacting defensively?

6. Why do you think we often categorize people as "allies" or "outsiders" based on how similar their beliefs are to ours? How does that mindset impact the way we love others?

Key Highlight:

Religion or some sort of belief system can be viewed as a contract, regarding individuals as mere objects to fulfill personal desires. Relationships within this context tend to be formed based on shared beliefs and like-mindedness. If someone does not share the same beliefs, the relationship often falters, and an invitation to connect is not extended. This perspective can extend into the workplace, where individuals are often assessed through a similar lens.

Colleagues are viewed as contracts—either allies or adversaries. Connections are formed with those who can help fulfill our ambitions, governed by our habits and goals.

With every contract comes an expectation of work; without effort, the contract loses its value. When we evaluate others through this lens, we may focus on their shortcomings, leading us to grumble, complain, or even condemn them. Our perceptions of others are often colored by our beliefs and habits. If we work hard to achieve success, we may expect the same from those around us. If we find peace in particular choices or behaviors, we may believe that others should also find their path in the same way. This mindset can create a rigid framework for understanding relationships, often neglecting the complexities of individual experiences and circumstances.

7. Do you find it easier to connect with people who share your beliefs or goals? What makes it difficult to build relationships with those who don't?

8. In what ways can ambition or performance-driven environments cause us to lose sight of someone's worth as God sees them?

9. Why is it often easier to judge others when they fall short of our standards, rather than respond with grace like Jesus does? What would change if we asked God to help us see them as He does?

PRAYER

Lord, Help me see people the way You see them—not as means to an end, but as deeply loved. Keep me from a religious mindset that focuses on performance over relationship.

Give me eyes to see, ears to hear, and hearts that reflect Your compassion and grace. In Jesus' name, Amen.

DEEPER THOUGHT AND DISCUSSION

It is easy to slip into a mindset where relationships feel transactional based on agreement, usefulness, or performance. This mirrors a religious approach, where people must meet certain expectations to be valued.

But Jesus calls us to something deeper: to see people as He does—loved, valuable, and worth pursuing no matter what they offer in return. Like Peter, our perspective often needs to shift from self-interest to compassion, from reaction to relationship. Who is God calling you to see differently?

Personal Study Day 3

OVERVIEW:

Like us, Peter, Andrew, James, and John grew up in a society that taught them to view others through a legalistic lens. However, Jesus challenged this worldview. In *Matthew 4:18-19*, as He walked along the shores of Galilee, He encountered these disciples and invited them to follow Him, saying, *"I will make you fishers of men."* It is likely that they were puzzled by His words, yet in verse 20, we see their immediate response: they left their nets and followed Him without hesitation.

In hindsight, we recognize that the disciples were somewhat slow learners; Jesus had to continually remind them of their purpose and responsibilities. Unlearning bad habits takes time, they grew up in a culture that shaped their thinking, leading them to see people through a very different lens. Seeing others as Jesus does was foreign to them—much like it is for many of us before we surrendered our lives to Jesus.

Ecclesiastes 3:11 (NIV) He has made everything beautiful in its time. He has also set eternity in the human heart; yet no one can fathom what God has done from beginning to end.

PERSONAL APPLICATION:

Key Highlight:

Jesus challenged his disciples to cultivate relationships with others, just as He has built a relationship with each of them. Instead of viewing people through a transactional lens, they are called to see them in the context of relationships. We are to recognize those who are lost, searching for guidance, and those who are hurting, in need of peace. In doing this, we shift our focus away from our self-worth tied to jobs, degrees, or talents—an outlook that promotes a contractual way of living.

Instead, we are encouraged to see our jobs, our degrees, and our gifts as byproducts of our relationship with God. As *Matthew 6:33* teaches us, *"But seek first the kingdom of God and his righteousness, and all these things will be added to you."* The emphasis here is not on securing the next contract, job, or relationship, but rather on seeking God above all else. From this foundation, we will begin to see people, our occupations, and our self-worth through the lens of our relationship with Him.

1. Think about someone in your life who may be lost, hurting, or searching. What would it look like to approach them as Jesus would—with compassion rather than an agenda?

2. Have you ever struggled to separate your self-worth from your job title, academic success, or gifts? How can Matthew 6:33 reshape that perspective?

Key Highlight:

Being a "fisher of men" does not necessarily mean we abandon our jobs and drop our nets, as the disciples did, unless God specifically calls us into full-time ministry. For some, this may indeed be the path God has for them, but the deeper lesson Jesus was imparting to His disciples goes beyond their means of making a living. He was revealing that life with Him transforms our entire worldview and approach to challenges.

Consider the story of Peter, who, after a night of unsuccessful fishing, received a directive from Jesus to cast his nets once more. *"Simon answered, 'Master, we have worked hard all night and have not caught anything. But because you say so, I will let down the nets.'" (Luke 5:5 NIV)*. This illustrates the concept of surrendering our plans and our understandings to Gods wisdom above what we perceive to be true. *Proverbs 3:5-6 tells us to "Trust in the Lord with all our heart and lean not on our own understanding; and in all our ways to acknowledge Him, and He will make our paths straight."*

Without an intimate relationship with Jesus, we cannot hear His guidance or perceive the world through His eyes. As we draw closer to Him, we start to understand His direction and see life as He sees it.

3. What does being a "fisher of men" look like in your current season of life? How might God be using your everyday responsibilities as part of His greater purpose?

4. What do Proverbs 3:5—6 and Luke 5:5 teach us about obedience even when things don't make sense? How do they challenge your current mindset or routines?

5. What steps can you take this week to lean less on your own understanding and more on God's direction—even in the small, daily decisions?

Key Highlight:

To be a true fisher of men, we must recognize that once we accept the call of God, we are called to die to our previous ways of thinking and let go of the habits that have caused our troubles leading up to our point of conversion. As disciples of Christ, if we fail to develop the ability to see people and circumstances from God's perspective, we cannot fully embrace the obedience to which He calls us. Our lives are no longer solely about us; they are about God and His work in the world.

Remember again *Matthew 6:33*, which states, *"But seek first His kingdom and His righteousness, and all these things will be given to you as well."* When our priorities align with God's purpose, we can confidently navigate life's challenges, trusting that He will provide for our needs and guide us in every step we take. God knows all things and sees the big picture. He is the one who does the hard work; our role is simply to let Him lead.

6. How do you respond to the idea that your life is no longer about you, but about God's work in the world? How can this shift in focus impact your daily choices and actions?

7. How can trusting that God sees the "big picture" help you navigate life's uncertainties or challenges? What areas in your life do you need to surrender to His guidance and timing?

PRAYER

Lord, help me surrender my old ways of thinking and prioritize Your kingdom above all else. Teach me to see people and circumstances through Your eyes, so I can follow Your lead and become a true "fisher of men."

Guide my steps, trusting that You hold the big picture and will provide for all my needs. May my life reflect Your purpose and bring glory to Your name, not my own. In Jesus' name, Amen.

DEEPER THOUGHT AND DISCUSSION

- How can we ensure that our discipleship efforts are not merely religious actions done out of obligation, but genuine acts of obedience and surrender?
- What are some practical ways to cultivate a heart of surrender and trust in the Holy Spirit rather than relying on control and legalism?

Personal Study Day 4

OVERVIEW:

The Bible says, *"The harvest is plentiful, but the laborers are few" (Matthew 9:37).* One of the main reasons for this is that many followers of Christ lack the eyes to see those in need. Right now, millions of individuals are experiencing hardships, and God is at work in their lives, drawing them to seek answers and understand their purpose in this world. Many can be found in bars, strip joints, and drug-infested alleys, while others are in front of a TV, drowning their sorrows in entertainment.

Romans 15:13 (NIV) - May the God of hope fill you with all joy and peace as you trust in him, so that you may overflow with hope by the power of the Holy Spirit.

PERSONAL APPLICATION

Key Highlight:

People who are lost are searching for individuals who see them as God sees them, not looking for judgment but for unconditional love. Many have never encountered the love of Christ in the way we have, and they remain unaware of what they are missing. Their past experiences with religion have often resulted in more heartache rather than healing. Unfortunately, they have been hurt as deeply by those in the church as they have by anyone else in their lives. Having only experienced transactional relationships, they have yet to know what it feels like to be in a relationship that is free from judgment and focuses solely on uplifting them.

1. What are some practical ways you can demonstrate God's love to someone who has been hurt by religion or the church?

2. How can you help someone understand the unconditional love of Christ when they have been hurt by others in the past?

Key Highlight:

Let's face it, hurt people often hurt others, and most of us have experienced some form of pain. Many are unable to resolve their feelings, which leads them down dark paths. Some bury themselves in work, making achievement their goal, yet inside they are hurting and yearning for answers, desperately seeking relief from the depression that perpetually knocks at their door.

God has an answer for all of this. He raises up an army of followers who see people as He sees them. His heart breaks for those who suffer; He sacrificed His life for them. As it says in *John 3:16, "For God so loved the world that he gave His one and only Son."* There is nothing He will not do for them, and He desires for us to love them as He does.

3. How have you seen the cycle of hurt—where hurt people hurt others—play out in your own life or the lives of those around you? How can we break that cycle?

4. What are some of the ways people may bury their pain (such as through work or achievement)? How can we recognize and address this pain in others?

5. How can you be a part of God's army, raising others up by seeing them through His eyes and showing compassion instead of judgment?

Key Highlight:

As followers of Christ, we no longer have to wrestle with hurt and past pains. God promises in *1 Peter 5:7, "Cast all your anxiety on him because he cares for you."* He takes away our struggles, giving us hope and purpose. He provides for all our needs and restores us to fullness in Christ. As *Galatians 2:20 says, "I have been crucified with Christ and I no longer live, but Christ lives in me."*

We now have the ability to view our circumstances through His eyes, trusting that He is working all things together for our good, as mentioned in Romans 8:28. With peace, joy, and alignment with God's perfect will, we become His warriors and agents of change.

6. What does it mean to "cast all your anxiety on Him" (1 Peter 5:7)? How can you apply this in your daily life when you feel overwhelmed or burdened?

7. What does it look like to be a "warrior" or an "agent of change" for God in your own life?

8. In what areas of your life are you still holding onto past pain or anxiety? How can you release those things to God, knowing He cares for you?

> **PRAYER**
>
> Lord, Thank You for the promise that I can cast all my anxieties on You because You care for me. Help me to trust You more deeply, releasing past hurts and struggles into Your hands. I am no longer defined by my pain or circumstances, but by my identity in Christ.
>
> Guide me to see life through Your eyes, trusting that You are working all things together for my good. Empower me to live with peace, joy, and purpose, becoming a warrior for Your kingdom and a vessel of Your love. - In Jesus' name, Amen.

DEEPER THOUGHT AND DISCUSSION

Hurt People Hurt Others: Many people carry pain and unresolved struggles, and hurt people often hurt others. When we experience hurt, it's easy to lash out or become defensive. But as followers of Christ, we are called to help those who are hurting, showing them the unconditional love of Jesus. Just as God heals our wounds, we are to point others to Him for restoration.

1 Peter 5:7 calls us to cast all our anxieties on God, offering us peace instead of burdens. Yet, we often hold on to anxiety because we think we must handle everything ourselves. Letting go means trusting that God cares for us and that He is in control, giving us the freedom to surrender our struggles to Him.

Personal Study Day 5

OVERVIEW:

God is at work. He sees the bigger picture and is continuously active around you. In the midst of your circumstances, ask Him to give you eyes to see His presence. God is focused on building relationships, and our attention should not be on the things beyond our control.

Proverbs 3:5–6 (NIV) Trust in the Lord with all your heart and lean not on your own understanding; in all your ways submit to him, and he will make your paths straight.

PERSONAL APPLICATION

Key Highlight:

You are in your current situation because He has entrusted you with a greater responsibility. As His child and a saint of God, you have been placed there to bring Him glory. Reflect on your upbringing and cultural influences in light of God's Word, always asking yourself, "How does God see this?"

Scripture serves as your greatest weapon against cultural bias. As *Hebrews 4:12* reminds us, *"For the word of God is alive and active. Sharper than any double-edged sword, it penetrates even to dividing soul and spirit, joints and marrow; it judges the thoughts and attitudes of the heart."* Memorize it and let go of religious rituals that might distract you from listening to God.

1. How does recognizing that you are in your current situation because God has entrusted you with greater responsibility change your perspective on your circumstances?

2. Reflect on your upbringing and cultural influences. Are there any beliefs or practices that conflict with God's Word? How can you begin to align your mindset with God's truth?

3. How can you deepen your engagement with reading God's word so it becomes your primary tool in navigating life and making decisions?

Key Highlight:

Turn to Him first in everything; listen for His guidance rather than relying on YouTube experts or the well-meaning advice of friends with experience. Seek to understand what God is saying and what He wants you to do.

Begin practicing what you have learned in this chapter with your family. Choose to stop viewing them through a contractual lens, judging their faults, or condemning them for not meeting your expectations or ideas of what is best. Let go of operating solely from your own will and understanding.

4. When faced with a decision, how often do you turn to God first rather than relying on external sources like advice from friends or online resources?

5. How do you discern when God is speaking to you and leading you in a certain direction?

6. What are some practical steps you can take to stop seeing your family through a "contractual lens" and start seeing them through God's eyes?

<u>Key Highlight:</u>

Learn to slow down, be patient with people, and simplify your approach towards them. Start loving them as Jesus loves us. Trust their struggles to God, allowing Him to take control of their lives while you elevate them above yourself. If you can embrace this perspective with your family, you will be well on your way to seeing others in the world through God's eyes.

Choose today to act according to what God reveals to you through His Word and through prayer. With Jesus, it is always about relationships. Remember, your past darkness is behind you, and the pathway to your future shines brighter than ever when you begin to see people as Jesus sees them. Making disciples becomes a natural byproduct of our relationship with God. As He opens our eyes, we start to recognize the potential in others to become disciples who will, in turn, make more disciples.

7. How often do you find yourself rushing through interactions with others? How can you practice slowing down and being more patient with those around you, especially with your family?

8. When you see others struggling, how can you trust their burdens to God and allow Him to take control, rather than trying to fix or control their situation yourself?

9. What role does seeing others as potential disciples play in your daily interactions and in fulfilling the Great Commission?

PRAYER

Father God, I come before You today, asking for the grace to slow down and be patient with those around me, especially my family. Help me to love them as You love me—unconditionally and selflessly. Teach me to trust their struggles to You, knowing that You are in control and working in their lives.

Guide me to see people through Your eyes, to elevate them above myself, and to recognize the potential in others to become disciples. As I seek to live according to Your Word and in prayer, I ask that You help me act on what You reveal to me.

May my relationships reflect Your love, and may making disciples be a natural overflow of the relationship I have with You. Thank You for leading me out of darkness and into the light of Your purpose. In Jesus' name, Amen.

DEEPER THOUGHT AND DISCUSSION:

Jesus challenges us to shift from a transactional approach to relationships towards one grounded in love, patience, and trust in God's guidance. In a world that often values efficiency, productivity, and self-interest, Jesus calls us to slow down, to love unconditionally, and to trust Him with the struggles of others. This is not about fixing people, but about being present with them, elevating them above ourselves, and recognizing their inherent worth as God's creation.

Loving others as Jesus loves us means responding with grace and understanding, not judgment. It calls us to see beyond external behaviors and view people through God's eyes—seeing their potential, their struggles, and their need for healing. When we embrace this perspective, our relationships become a space for healing and growth, both for ourselves and those around us.

Finally, making disciples is a natural byproduct of living in this way. When we genuinely love and trust others, pointing them to Jesus, we create an environment where transformation can occur. By seeing people as God sees them, we not only help them on their journey but also grow deeper in our own relationship with Him. This is how God works through us to fulfill His purpose in the world.

Session 3 Eyes to See - Song

Song Title: Eyes to See

Eyes To See is a song of perspective—learning to see through the lens of heaven. When our eyes are fully surrendered, we no longer view people, purpose, or pain the same. We begin to see with compassion, clarity, and conviction.

As disciples, we're not just called to follow Jesus—we're called to see like Him. And as we lead others, we must teach them to fix their eyes not on the world, but on the One who leads us all.

Bible Verse:

"Turn my eyes from looking at worthless things; and give me life in your ways." —Psalm 119:37 (ESV)

🎵 🎵 **Scan the QR code to listen and ask the Lord to give you surrendered eyes that see as He sees.**

https://youtu.be/
igKcnQ4gJbk

Chapter 4

Session 4 Be Still and Equipped

To get the most out of your daily personal study, begin by reading the corresponding chapter from the book. This provides the context you will need to reflect deeply and answer the questions thoughtfully. While the study guide focuses on the first eight chapters—each divided into five sections for daily reflection—the book also includes four additional training chapters to further equip you.

Start each day in prayer, inviting the Holy Spirit to open your heart and show you what He wants you to see. As you work through the questions, do so with honesty, vulnerability, and humility. Let the Holy Spirit lead you, shape you, and bring lasting transformation through this journey.

OVERVIEW:

To truly understand Jesus, we must first commit ourselves to knowing Him. A strong relationship requires time and effort; without these, our relationship with Him will simply not flourish. So, what are the two primary factors that hinder us from cultivating a strong relationship with God, ultimately affecting how our lives reflect His calling?

First, we lack a consistent daily quiet time with God. Second, we are unequipped to study the Word of God at the level expected of a disciple. God calls all disciples to attain a deep and thorough understanding of all things Jesus, akin to earning a PhD in our faith.

2 Timothy 2:15 (ESV) - Do your best to present yourself to God as one approved, a worker who has no need to be ashamed, rightly handling the word of truth.

Personal Study Day 1

PERSONAL APPLICATION

Key Highlight:

Perhaps some reasons why these two factors hinder our ability to know Jesus more are that our lives are too busy, leaving little room for spiritual exploration. Or maybe we have lost interest, feeling that our connection with God no longer fulfills us. It could also be that we have become complacent, viewing the effort required to maintain this relationship as burdensome, or we prioritize other habits that seem more rewarding. Maybe life is comfortable, and everything is going smoothly—why pursue another relationship if it is not necessary? For some, past hurts from the Church may have created deep wounds, causing them to keep everything at arm's length. Any of these reasons can hinder our journey toward a closer relationship with Jesus.

1. Do you have any current habits or routines in your life that may be unintentionally crowding out your time with Jesus?

2. What would it look like to prioritize your relationship with Jesus over things that seem more rewarding or urgent?

Key Highlight:

In *Hebrews 5:12-14*, the writer reminds us, *"For though by this time you ought to be teachers, you need someone to teach you again the basic principles of the oracles of God. You need milk, not solid food, for everyone who lives on milk is unskilled in the word of righteousness, since he is a child. But solid food is for the mature, for those who have their powers of discernment trained by constant practice to distinguish good from evil."* By God's grace, we all should be moving beyond milk and are able to digest the rich, nourishing steak of God's word.

3. What does it mean to "move beyond milk" in your spiritual life?

4. What might "solid food" look like for you in this season of life?

5. How often do you spend intentional time in God's Word, seeking to go deeper in understanding and application?

Key Highlight:

As *Proverbs 16:3* reminds us, *"Commit to the Lord whatever you do, and he will establish your plans."* We discover God's plans when we are still before Him, and what we do during that quiet time is what He is telling us to do. Our paths should be guided by divine intention rather than personal ambition alone. A genuine relationship with God requires humility and a willingness to align our lives with His will. However, too often we allow our work, family, and hobbies to take up most of our time.

Recognizing the importance of making Jesus a priority in your life is crucial for safeguarding your ministry from becoming stale and lifeless. It is in the stillness of His presence that everything truly begins.

6. How does prioritizing Jesus influence the way you see your personal ministry, whether it's in your home, workplace, or church?

7. What steps can you take this week to realign your time and energy around God's will for your life?

PRAYER

Lord, I confess the times I've let busyness, comfort, or distractions pull me away from You. Help me hunger for more than spiritual milk—grow me into maturity through Your Word. Teach me to slow down, to be still in Your presence, and to trust Your plans above my own. I commit my life, my thoughts, and my time to You. Realign my heart with Yours and let my relationship with You always come first. Amen.

DEEPER THOUGHT AND DISCUSSION

Spiritual growth often stalls not because God is distant, but because we've allowed other priorities to crowd Him out. Whether it's comfort, past wounds, or daily responsibilities, we can easily drift into a shallow faith. But God invites us deeper. Just as we grow from milk to solid food, He calls us into maturity—where we learn to trust His plans, not just pursue our own. When we intentionally slow down and sit in His presence, we begin to hear His voice more clearly and see our lives through His eyes.

Personal Study Day 2

OVERVIEW:

After my awakening, God brought a verse to my heart from *Psalm 46:10*: *"Be still, and know that I am God."* This verse had a profound impact on my life because it highlighted one area where I was lacking in my daily walk with God: the practice of stillness. I had never taken the time to truly be still in God's presence—not just physically, but also mentally and spiritually.

I realized that I needed to engage in authentic communion with Him, like the quiet moments I share with my wife when we are alone, free from the distractions of the outside world. A relationship built amidst the chaos of life, with little to no time for meditation, is inherently unstable. Being still before God allows for a deeper connection, fostering a more solid and enduring relationship.

Mark 1:35 (NIV) - "Very early in the morning, while it was still dark, Jesus got up, left the house and went off to a solitary place, where he prayed."

PERSONAL APPLICATION:

Key Highlight:

In the beginning, I often found myself pondering what is required during quiet time with God. How long should it last? Will it be boring? Is it truly beneficial to slow down and simply be still in His presence? I had many questions for God because I genuinely wanted to understand His thoughts on all matters. A few insights He shared with me about the importance of being still before Him is that it teaches me to slow down and develop more patience in how I respond to the challenges of the outside world.

Psalm 37:7 comes to mind: *"Be still before the Lord and wait patiently for him; do not fret when people succeed in their ways, when they carry out their wicked schemes."* During my quiet time with God, I have discovered the ability to view people and my circumstances through His eyes. I hear His truth for my life in relation to whatever I am experiencing at that moment.

1. What doubts or hesitations have you had about spending quiet time with God?

2. How do you currently approach being still before God? What does that look like for you?

3. How could developing a habit of stillness help you see others and your circumstances through God's eyes?

Key Highlight:

Lamentations 3:25-26 echoes this sentiment: *"The Lord is good to those who wait for him, to the soul that seeks him. It is good that one should wait quietly for the salvation of the Lord."* I can personally attest to the truth of this verse; waiting on God has brought peace to my soul and fulfillment to my ministry that I have never known before. Something transformative occurs deep within you when you carve out quiet time with God.

In *1 Peter 1:16*, God calls us to "be holy because He is holy." Understanding God's holiness is a profound journey, and R.C. Sproul's book, "The Holiness of God", can be a valuable resource in helping you grasp this concept. I struggled with this idea for a long time, especially before I committed to a consistent quiet time with God, during which I often fell into temptation.

4. What are some ways you have experienced transformation during your quiet time with God?

5. What role does holiness play in your relationship with God, and how does it impact your spiritual growth?

6. *Lamentations 3:25-26* says that it is *"good that one should wait quietly for the salvation of the Lord."* How do you interpret this in the context of your own spiritual journey?

Key Highlight:

After consistent quiet time with God noticeable changes occur. Months later, I found myself resisting Satan's traps much more effectively. This transformation recalls *1 Corinthians 10:13*, which states, *"No temptation has overtaken you except what is common to mankind. And God is faithful; he will not let you be tempted beyond what you can bear. But when you are tempted, he will also provide a way out so that you can endure it."* Through my quiet time, I became more aware of these escape routes and was no longer blinded by my own foolishness.

Another change I noticed was that I stopped complaining and gossiping about others as much, becoming more aware that God is in control and allowing me to rest in Him. I realized I did not need to complain about everything; instead, I could speak life and trust God with all things. As *James 5:9* reminds us, *"Don't grumble against one another, brothers and sisters, or you will be judged. The Judge is standing at the door!"*

7. 1 Corinthians 10:13 speaks of God providing a way out of temptation. How have you experienced this in your own life through your quiet time with God?

8. James 5:9 warns against grumbling. How does trusting God in all things help you stop complaining and begin speaking life over situations and others?

PRAYER

Lord, I thank You for the transformative power of quiet time with You. Help me to be still before You, to patiently wait on Your guidance, and to trust that You are working in my life. I ask for Your strength to resist temptation and to recognize the escape routes You provide when I face trials. May I be more aware of Your holiness and learn to speak life, not grumbling or complaining. Teach me to rest in Your control and find peace in trusting You with all things. Guide me to consistently make time for You so that I can grow in faith and be more like You each day.

In Jesus' name, Amen.

DEEPER THOUGHT AND DISCUSSION

When we consistently spend quiet time with God, it reshapes the way we live and respond to the world around us. At first, the discipline may seem unfamiliar or even difficult—but over time, it becomes a space where transformation happens. In stillness, we begin to hear God more clearly, respond with greater patience, and see people through His eyes instead of reacting out of our flesh.

This time with Him strengthens our spiritual discernment, helping us recognize and avoid temptation more easily. It also humbles us, softening our hearts so we complain less, gossip less, and trust more. The quiet moments develop holiness in us—not as a task to perform, but as a response to being in His presence.

The more we slow down with God, the more we begin to reflect Him in how we live. It's in that space of stillness that real maturity is formed. What once felt like a religious duty becomes a place of deep connection, peace, and power.

Personal Study Day 3

OVERVIEW:

One practice that has worked particularly well for me is rising early to spend time with Him. This quiet time in the morning sets a positive tone for my entire day. Martin Luther once said that when he was especially busy, he felt compelled to spend at least three hours in prayer to get everything done. *Mark 1:35* supports this practice that Jesus teaches us: *"And rising very early in the morning, while it was still dark, he departed and went out to a desolate place, and there he prayed."*

Psalm 5:3 (NIV) - "In the morning, Lord, you hear my voice; in the morning I lay my requests before you and wait expectantly."

PERSONAL APPLICATION:

Key Highlight:

Jesus demonstrated that getting up early to spend time with God is of utmost importance. Like Martin Luther, when we find ourselves very busy, we may need to dedicate ample time early in the morning to cast all our burdens onto God while also creating space to simply listen to Him.

Find a quiet place in your home or somewhere free from distractions. As it states in *Luke 5:16*, *"Jesus often withdrew to lonely places and prayed."* Whether it is your closet, garage, or back patio, establishing this habit of being still will radically change your life. A disciple follows Jesus' example, and this was His daily practice, so it should be ours as well.

1. Why do you think Jesus made it a priority to withdraw and pray early in the morning?

2. How might your perspective or day shift if you started early in the morning by surrendering your burdens and simply listening to God?

3. How do you respond to the idea that the busier your life gets, the more time you should spend with God, not less?

<u>Key Highlight:</u>

Just like us, Jesus faced opposition from the enemy, and He recognized the need for the Father to fight for Him. He understood the message of *Exodus 14:14*, which says, *"The Lord will fight for you; you need only to be still."* We cannot win our battles without God fighting for us, and the Bible makes it clear that for the Lord to fight for us, we must first be still.

Never engage in battles that are outside of your control. First and foremost, recognize them as spiritual conflicts. As *Ephesians 6:12* (NIV) states, *"For our struggle is not against flesh and blood, but against the rulers, against the authorities, against the powers of this dark world and against the spiritual forces of evil in the heavenly realms."* Our victory is found daily on our knees in prayer, as each day brings new challenges. We must consistently cast all our anxieties onto God, for He cares for us, as expressed in 1 Peter 5:7. Being consistently still in God's presence is essential if we are to become fruitful disciples.

4. How can you recognize when a situation is a spiritual battle rather than just a physical or emotional one?

5. How can verses like Exodus 14:14 and Ephesians 6:12 shift your perspective when you're facing opposition?

6. What are some practical ways you can develop the habit of bringing your anxieties to God in prayer?

Key Highlight:

The Bible teaches us that the strength to endure comes from resting and finding quietness before the Lord. As *Isaiah 30:15* says, *"For thus said the Lord God, the Holy One of Israel: 'In returning and rest you shall be saved; in quietness and trust shall be your strength.'"*

I can personally testify that everything in my life changed for the better when I made it a priority to be still in God's presence each day. A disciple of God can do nothing without remaining in the vine, as John 15:5 tells us; that connection begins in stillness. We cannot be disciple-makers if we do not have this kind of relationship with Jesus.

You can always recognize a true disciple of God because they possess a distinctiveness that sets them apart. One consistent truth among all of them is that they prioritize quality quiet time with God. If you are not currently making this time for Him, I highly encourage you to make a change—starting today!

7. How does John 15:5 speak to your connection with God and your effectiveness as a disciple?

8. What qualities have you observed in people who consistently spend time in God's presence, and how can you begin to model that?

9. What is one specific step you can take this week to deepen your daily time alone with God that you have not already done?

> **PRAYER**
>
> Lord, Thank You for the quiet moments that draw me closer to You. Teach me to slow down, to make space in my day to be still before You. I need Your strength, not my own. Help me to recognize my battles as spiritual and trust that You are fighting for me. Root me deeply in Your presence so that I can walk with wisdom, speak with grace, and love like You. Make me a disciple who abides fully in You each day.
>
> In Jesus' name, amen.

DEEPER THOUGHT AND DISCUSSION

Jesus modeled what it means to prioritize quiet time with the Father—even in the middle of a busy and demanding life. His consistent practice of withdrawing to pray wasn't just for rest, it was for realignment. In stillness, we remember who we are and who God is.

When we neglect time alone with God, we often begin to fight battles in our own strength, reacting to life rather than responding in wisdom. But when we sit with Him, we gain clarity, peace, and the strength to endure. Our confidence grows—not because life gets easier, but because we're rooted in Someone greater.

Discipleship does not begin with striving; it begins with stillness. That daily connection with God is what sets true disciples apart. If we want to live like Jesus, we must also love the quiet like He did.

Personal Study Day 4

OVERVIEW:

In high school, I was the typical athlete who cared more about sports and girls than academics. I loathed reading and was quite adept at convincing others to do my homework for me. Sure, I would study the night before a test and, to my surprise, usually manage to do fairly well. But studying felt like pulling teeth; it was something I simply could not enjoy. I am sure some of you in regards to studying can relate to my sentiments, but many of you likely thrive on studying, effortlessly soaking up knowledge. For me, studying would have been an act of God.

When college came around, not much changed; studying was still a bore—until one day, everything shifted. I was a pitcher in baseball, and everything changed right after I pitched a nine-inning game where I struck out multiple batters and felt like the king of the world. In a moment of pride, I even declared, "I'm so good, I'm like God." Yes, I really said that, and in that moment, God did something profound within me. The very next day, the desire to compete in sports vanished. I cannot explain it other than to say that after practice the next day, I grabbed my gear and walked away, never looking back. Right then, I heard God calling me into ministry.

Galatians 6:3 (ESV) - "For if anyone thinks he is something, when he is nothing, he deceives himself."

PERSONAL APPLICATION

Key Highlight:

At that time, I was newly married with a child on the way, and something changed inside me. I began to study. This was nothing short of miraculous—suddenly, I could not get enough of God. His grace overwhelmed me. I knew I did not deserve His favor, yet I felt His goodness in my life. I devoured everything I could find, listening to sermons constantly. The wealth of knowledge I gained in such a short time was remarkable; I truly felt reborn. I took my calling seriously and strived to be the best student of God's Word that I could be.

1. Have you ever experienced a moment when God stirred something new in your heart? What did that look like?

2. Why do you think grace—especially when we know we don't deserve it—can be such a powerful motivator for transformation?

Key Highlight:

Looking back now, I can see there was a problem: I had not fully surrendered my life to God. I still yearned for wealth and sought to experience life based on my own desires. I was the typical legalistic pastor, brimming with knowledge but devoid of love and genuine obedience. I share this because I know many people have fallen into the same trap. As 1 *Corinthians 8:1* reminds us, *"Knowledge puffs up, but love builds up."*

I was the one who puffed up rather than built up. I was also the type of person who justified my life, convincing myself that I was loving others and walking closely with God. But deep down, I was miserable. On the outside, I was kind to people, unless someone with intellect threatened me; then, I became a different person. I used my knowledge to condemn others in an effort to make myself appear smarter. I frequently gave presentations to showcase how intelligent I was but rarely engaged in conversations where both sides were equally valued.

3. Have you ever recognized a time in your life when you were outwardly "spiritual" but inwardly far from surrendering fully to God?

4. What does it mean to truly surrender your desires to God—and why is that so difficult at times?

5. Reflect on 1 Corinthians 8:1. How can we shift from being puffed up with knowledge to building others up in love?

6. Have you ever used spiritual knowledge to justify behavior that wasn't aligned with Christ's character? What did you learn from that?

7. In your relationships or leadership, are there signs that pride or the desire to appear "right" may be getting in the way of truly connecting with others?

Key Highlight:

In *Matthew 16:26*, Jesus tells His disciples, *"What good will it be for someone to gain the whole world, yet forfeit their soul?"* I was accumulating knowledge for my own benefit while living a double life. I presented myself as a good Christian in public, yet behind closed doors, I was serving myself in sin. I became painfully aware of my own fraudulence; my studying was driven by how I wanted others to perceive me.

It was only later that God revealed to me the true purpose of my study: it should be in alignment with obedience and reverence for Him. My learning needed to revolve around decreasing so that He could increase. In my quiet moments, I now find myself broken and contrite before God. Any knowledge I gain is meant for His glory—it never pertains to me but rather to the purposes He has for me. What comes naturally now is my deep desire to be equipped and prepared for the battles I face each day.

Accompanying our quiet time with God is our meditation on His Word, engaging with His truth. One distinctive feature of a true disciple is their deep knowledge of Scripture—not simply possessing information, but practicing obedience based on that knowledge. When God speaks to a disciple, a fruit-bearing disciple responds with obedience and makes the necessary adjustments in their life.

8. In what ways can the pursuit of knowledge become self-serving rather than God-honoring?

9. Have you ever found yourself more focused on how others perceive your faith rather than how God sees your heart?

10. How would you define a "fruit-bearing disciple," and are there areas in your life where more fruit is needed?

11. What's one area where God is calling you to not just gain knowledge, but act in obedience?

> **PRAYER**
>
> Lord, thank You for drawing me closer to You, even when my motives have not always been pure. I confess the times I sought knowledge for my own pride or approval rather than to honor You. Forgive me for the moments I appeared faithful on the outside while hiding compromise within. I surrender my heart fully to You now—my study, my thoughts, my desires. Let everything I learn lead me to deeper obedience and love. Teach me to decrease, so that You may increase in every part of my life. Help me walk humbly, serve faithfully, and bear fruit that brings You glory. Amen.

DEEPER THOUGHT AND DISCUSSION

It's possible to be deeply involved in ministry, passionate about studying God's Word, and still be disconnected from the heart of God. Many begin their spiritual journey with enthusiasm and hunger, but without full surrender, that hunger can subtly shift into self-glorification. Knowledge without humility breeds pride, and pride distances us from the very God we claim to serve.

This journey reminds us that studying Scripture is not about appearance or achievement—it's about transformation. It's not about how much we know but how much we're changed. As Jesus said in Matthew 16:26, gaining everything—recognition, knowledge, influence—means nothing if we lose our soul in the process.

True discipleship is marked not just by learning, but by obedience. When we are confronted with truth, we must be willing to make the hard adjustments, to allow God to prune us, and to let His Word reshape us. The goal is never information, but intimacy with Jesus that results in real, lasting fruit.

Personal Study Day 5

OVERVIEW:

To be adequately equipped, one must be a dedicated student of Scripture, possessing a deep hunger to know everything about God. Studying should become as instinctive as breathing. A transformed life is always ready to share the reason for its hope, as *1 Peter 3:15* states: *"But in your hearts revere Christ as Lord. Always be prepared to give an answer to everyone who asks you to give the reason for the hope that you have. But do this with gentleness and respect."*

This verse has inspired many Christian apologists to prepare thoughtful defenses of their faith. However, it is important to note that Peter is not addressing only those with the gift of apologetics. He speaks to believers who are facing persecution for their faith, emphasizing that all Christians should be ready to articulate what they believe and why.

2 Timothy 3:16-17 (NIV) - "All Scripture is God-breathed and is useful for teaching, rebuking, correcting and training in righteousness, so that the servant of God may be thoroughly equipped for every good work."

PERSONAL APPLICATION

Key Highlight:

Some disciples who take this calling to heart may develop a sense of superiority, mistakenly believing that their extensive knowledge of the Bible and God elevates them above others, as I once did. This attitude can lead to legalism and self-righteousness in their demeanor. Yet, Peter reminds us that our defense should be rooted in gentleness and respect, accompanied by a clear conscience.

In *Ephesians 4:15*, Paul echoes this sentiment, urging believers to embody Christ's teachings by *"speaking the truth in love."* Peter also shares that the reason why we speak the truth in love is because for those who speak maliciously against our good behavior in Christ may ultimately feel ashamed of their slander (1 Peter 3:16).

1. Why do you think it is so easy to slip into legalism or self-righteousness as we grow in our faith?

2. How do Peter's words in 1 Peter 3:16 challenge the way we defend our beliefs?

3. What does it look like to "speak the truth in love" in your own life, especially when dealing with difficult conversations?

Key Highlight:

To have an intimate relationship with God, one must internalize His words, as David expressed in *Psalm 119:11: "I have hidden your word in my heart that I might not sin against you."* We are called to be doers of the Word, not merely hearers (James 1:22). A true disciple memorizes God's Word through study and actively implements what they learn; without this practice, one cannot truly call themselves a disciple.

Now, what about those who dislike reading? I hear this often, and to them, I suggest bringing it before the Lord. Ask Him how He would like you to address this feeling. The Bible clearly emphasizes the importance of lifelong dedication to learning. *Proverbs 19:8* states, *"Do yourself a favor and learn all you can; then remember what you learn, and you will prosper."* Similarly, in *Proverbs 4:13*, we read, *"Always remember what you have learned. Your education is your life—guard it well."* These verses, penned by Solomon, the wisest man, highlight that learning and application are of utmost importance.

If reading poses a challenge for you, ask God to help you find a new perspective on it, just as He did for me. It truly was a miracle to discover my ability to read as much as I do now. While I know audiobooks can be helpful, physical reading, especially of the Bible, should remain a priority. I always make notes in my Bible and underline key verses, such as *Matthew 11:29: "Take my yoke upon you and learn from me."*

4. James 1:22 says we are to *"be doers of the Word."* What is one way you've recently acted on something you read in Scripture?

5. Have you ever struggled with reading the Bible or staying consistent in study? What helped you overcome that, or what still feels like a barrier?

6. What does it mean to you to "hide God's Word in your heart"? How have you practiced this in your own walk with Him?

Key Highlight:

Jesus set the example for us to be still in God's presence daily and to know His Word intimately. He consistently reminded people of what Scripture says, even confronting Satan directly during His confrontation with him as we find in (Mathew 4:1-11, Mark 1:12-13, Luke 4:1-13). Jesus taught us that having God's Word etched in your heart, you can wield a defense against the devil's schemes.

Each day in Christ presents a fresh opportunity to bring Him glory. We achieve this by intentionally spending time in His presence and immersing ourselves in His Word, allowing it to guide and transform us.

The knowledge we gain through our studies is meant to help others overcome obstacles that may be hindering them from coming to Jesus. It is not intended to condemn, but to build up and guide people into a loving relationship with Him. As *Romans 15:4* reminds us, *"For everything that was written in the past was written to teach us, so that through the endurance taught in the Scriptures and the encouragement they provide, we might have hope."* Being equipped and obedient to Gods word not only strengthens our own faith but also provides hope for those we disciple.

7. How does Jesus' example of using Scripture to confront Satan challenge or inspire the way you approach spiritual battles?

8. How can your time in God's Word today help equip you to disciple others tomorrow?

9. Romans 15:4 speaks of Scripture providing endurance and hope. How have you experienced this personally in your own journey?

PRAYER

Lord, Thank You for the example You set in Scripture and for showing us how to be still in Your presence. Help me to make time each day to draw near to You, to immerse myself in Your Word, and to allow it to shape my heart and mind. May I use the knowledge I gain not to elevate myself, but to build others up in love and truth. Teach me how to wield Your Word as a defense against the enemy and to live with intentionality, bringing glory to You in everything I do. Strengthen my faith and help me share the hope and encouragement I find in Your Scriptures with others. In Jesus' name, Amen.

DEEPER THOUGHT AND DISCUSSION:

Stillness in God's Presence:

Jesus shows us the importance of withdrawing from distractions to spend time with God. This quiet time allows us to hear His voice, lay down our worries, and align with His will. In a busy world, stillness is essential to discern God's guidance, and it strengthens our relationship with Him.

Internalizing and Obeying God's Word:

True disciples hide God's Word in their hearts, not just to gain knowledge, but to protect themselves from sin and apply it in everyday life. Knowledge must lead to obedience, as Jesus teaches that wisdom comes from both hearing and doing His Word. Consistent study, even when difficult, brings growth and wisdom.

Using God's Word to Build Others Up:

Jesus used Scripture to resist temptation, showing us how God's Word equips us to face challenges. It's not just for our benefit but to help others find hope in Christ. Scripture encourages and strengthens both us and those we disciple, guiding them toward faith and truth.

In short, being a disciple means spending time with God, truly internalizing His Word, and using it to serve others in love, growing in our faith, and helping others grow as well.

Chapter 4 Be Still and Equipped - Songs

Song Title: All of Me, All for You

There is a sacred moment when we finally stop striving and simply surrender—all that we are, for all that He is. All of Me, All for You is a prayer of stillness and devotion, laying down distractions to be fully present with God. It's in that stillness that we're reshaped, renewed, and equipped for the mission ahead.

Bible Verse:

"Be still, and know that I am God..."—Psalm 46:10a (NIV)

♫ ♫ **Scan the QR code to listen and offer your whole heart, quiet, surrendered, and ready.**

https://youtu.be/
ENgOjgTvFmA

Chapter 5

Session 5 Setting the Bar High

To get the most out of your daily personal study, begin by reading the corresponding chapter from the book. This provides the context you will need to reflect deeply and answer the questions thoughtfully. While the study guide focuses on the first eight chapters—each divided into five sections for daily reflection—the book also includes four additional training chapters to further equip you.

Start each day in prayer, inviting the Holy Spirit to open your heart and show you what He wants you to see. As you work through the questions, do so with honesty, vulnerability, and humility. Let the Holy Spirit lead you, shape you, and bring lasting transformation through this journey.

Personal Study Day 1

OVERVIEW:

To embrace this new life and rise beyond ordinary, we must cultivate new habits and establish systems that reflect God's truth.

To pursue God is to pursue the very best that life has to offer. Everything about God is good and perfect. Once we experience His deep love for us in this way, dying to our old way of life becomes a natural choice—why would we ever settle for anything less than His best?

I know the enemy often tries to make us feel condemned, as if we are not good enough. After reading through some of the previous chapters, it is easy to feel like we are not doing enough, and now we come to a chapter that challenges us to set the bar even higher. But the truth is, God is not condemning you. He simply wants your heart and a sincere desire to live a life of purpose for His glory. As it says in *Romans 8:1*, *"There is therefore now no condemnation for those who are in Christ Jesus."* Every day is a new opportunity to walk in His grace, to bask in His glory, and to live life to the fullest, in alignment with His will.

Galatians 2:20 (ESV): "I have been crucified with Christ. It is no longer I who live, but Christ who lives in me. And the life I now live in the flesh I live by faith in the Son of God, who loved me and gave himself for me."

PERSONAL APPLICATION

Key Highlight:

I am a huge sports fan and love the thrill of competition. What makes sports enjoyable is seeing two disciplined and skilled teams or individuals face off against each other. Can you imagine how different the games would be if the athletes did not put forth their best effort in training? If they were not fully committed to being the very best, you would have to ask yourself if they are truly pursuing their calling and whether they should continue competing.

This mirrors life: we can either coast along, merely getting by without challenging ourselves, or we can discover our calling and strive to excel in it. Too often, many people drift through life with little discipline, living without purpose. They become complainers, content with a status quo that demands little to no sacrifice. These individuals have typically never been challenged to raise the bar, nor have they encountered alternatives that inspire them to live differently. They may lack the skills to achieve greatness or simply lack the opportunity to make a difference.

1. How does the discipline and dedication seen in athletes challenge your own approach to your calling in life and faith?

2. In what areas of your life do you find yourself "coasting" instead of striving for excellence?

3. Who in your life has inspired you to "raise the bar" in your walk with God or your personal growth?

Key Highlight:

On the other end of the spectrum, we find those who are making a positive impact but are filled with pride. They possess the necessary skills and opportunities to do remarkable things, and they seize every opportunity. Nevertheless, their motivation is often self-serving; they operate in their own strength and can become defensive when challenged, often reminding others of their successes.

God loves both groups equally but would not choose either in their current state to be His disciples. They fail to see their lives from God's perspective and do not understand that we were created to glorify Him, and not to fulfill our own desires. Until an individual reaches the end of themselves and submits their life fully to God's way, they cannot truly be His disciple.

4. Have you ever found yourself serving or leading with pride rather than humility? What did that look like?

5. Why do you think it's so easy for success to shift our focus from glorifying God to glorifying ourselves?

6. Why is full surrender to God's way essential for true discipleship?

7. Can you think of a time when someone's humility had a greater impact on you than their talent or success?

Key Highlight:

God sets a high standard, and He expects us to live up to this calling. The Bible teaches that we are either for Him or against Him; being lukewarm will lead to God wanting to vomit you out of His mouth, as stated in Revelation 3:16. Unfortunately, many within the church today who practice religion find themselves in this middle ground. These are not the people we want to invest our time in for making disciples.

We must set the bar high for our lives and seek individuals who are like-minded and are Faithful, Available, and Teachable. If someone does not embody a heart seeking God in surrender or show a genuine desire for a deep relationship with Him, why should we invest our time in them, especially when God Himself has said He would "vomit" them out of His mouth? Furthermore, how can we call ourselves true disciples if we are living a double life? The truth is, we cannot.

8. Why do you think many people settle into a lukewarm faith, and how can we guard ourselves from falling into that pattern?

9. How can we discern if someone is truly seeking God versus just going through the motions of religion?

10. What does it look like to "set the bar high" in your personal walk with God?

PRAYER

Lord, Thank You for calling me to a higher standard. Help me not to drift through life without purpose or to serve out of pride, but to live each day surrendered to Your will. I want to glorify You with every gift and opportunity You've given me. Purify my heart from any lukewarmness and give me the courage to live fully for You. Lead me to invest in people who are hungry for You, and make me faithful, available, and teachable in all things. Strengthen me to live a life that honors You—one of excellence, humility, and obedience. In Jesus' name, Amen.

DEEPER THOUGHT AND DISCUSSION

May we be challenged to examine our disciplines, motives, and authenticity as disciples. Like athletes, we must train intentionally in our walk with Christ—spiritual growth does not happen by accident.

Pride can sneak in when we see success, but God is not impressed by self-glorification. True discipleship comes from a surrendered, humble heart.

Jesus makes it clear in Revelation 3:16 that lukewarm faith is unacceptable. We are either all in or not in at all. We must pursue God wholeheartedly and invest in others who are ready to grow—those who are Faithful, Available, and Teachable.

Personal Study Day 2

OVERVIEW:

Word experts suggest that the idiom "set the bar high" began to be used around the turn of the twentieth century. It originates from the sport of track and field, specifically in events like the high jump and pole vault. In these competitions, the bar is raised incrementally, allowing athletes to see how high they can jump or vault.

This concept applies equally to our spiritual lives. *"Once we were lost, but now we are found," (Luke 15:24).* We do not remain in that lost state; instead, through our obedience to God, we gradually raise the bar incrementally in our spiritual journey. Each week, we uncover new truths about God and learn how to align our lives with His perfect will. As *Philippians 3:14* reminds us, *"I press on toward the goal to win the prize for which God has called me heavenward in Christ Jesus."*

Colossians 3:23-24 (ESV): - "Whatever you do, work heartily, as for the Lord and not for men, knowing that from the Lord you will receive the inheritance as your reward. You are serving the Lord Christ."

PERSONAL APPLICATION:

Key Highlight:

We remain steadfast, determined to finish the race strong. Our lives reflect high moral standards built on a foundation of excellence, as we strive to give our very best effort in all that we do. A notable company called Credera, which is a consulting firm with a

96% customer retention rate, actively seeks individuals who are overachievers, strive for growth, embrace challenges, and help others do the same. One of the hiring managers at the firm expressed that they are continually impressed by the brilliant, innovative, diligent, and highly skilled professionals they have the privilege of working alongside. They have made a commitment to set the bar high in whom they hire, they want only the best and the results speak for themselves.

How much more should we aspire to set the bar high in our relationship with God? Shouldn't we strive to give our best effort and live in obedience to the standards and calling He has placed on our lives? I believe we should. When we have an intimate relationship with God, it naturally empowers us to live this way for His glory. Our lives reflect His goodness, becoming a source of inspiration for others. Many will catch the fire we emit and will be drawn to follow the path God is leading us on.

1. What does it mean to you personally to "finish the race strong" in your walk with God?

2. How does your personal pursuit of excellence influence or inspire others around you?

3. What is one specific step you can take this week to give God your very best?

Key Highlight:

When seeking disciples to invest time with, we should focus on individuals who are genuinely pursuing God. We are not looking for perfect people; in fact, it is often the opposite. We will primarily find those who are broken and struggling with sin, just like we do. In our culture, unfortunately, we have redefined what it is to be called a Christian. We have lowered the bar so much!

In *Luke 14:25-33*, we read, *"Now great crowds were traveling with Jesus. So, He turned and said to them: 'If anyone comes to Me and does not hate his own father and mother, wife and children, brothers and sisters—yes, even his own life—he cannot be My disciple. Whoever does not bear his own cross and come after Me cannot be My disciple.'*

Here, Jesus is not setting an easily attainable standard; rather, He emphasizes that nothing in this world should take precedence over following Him. He calls us to eliminate distractions that could hinder our relationship with Him. The implication is clear: if we allow anything to stand in the way, we cannot truly be His disciples. The bar that Jesus sets for our lives is high, and lowering those standards is not something we should ever do for ourselves or for the disciples we are discipling.

4. How has our culture redefined what it means to be a Christian, and how do you see that affecting the church today?

5. Jesus sets a high standard for discipleship—how do you personally respond to that challenge?

6. When investing in others, what qualities do you look for to determine if someone is genuinely pursuing God?

Key Highlight:

Our purpose is to make disciples who make disciples, and if we engage with individuals who are not yet disciples, we limit the potential for multiplication.

From the start, we need to clearly communicate the cost of discipleship. Cast a vision for where you will go together and ensure they understand the commitment required to follow Jesus. Our desire should align with Jesus' desire: in His grace, we cultivate disciples who are deeply in love with Him, who bear fruit, love others as He loves them, and ultimately make more disciples. If they choose to move forward with you, we must maintain high standards and live a holy life before God.

Do not view raising the bar as an excuse for legalism. We all fall short, and we should always lean on the side of grace. Avoid becoming rigid or harsh; instead, show compassion, understanding that we are just as imperfect as anyone else. The key difference between a F.A.T. Christian pursuing a relationship with Jesus and a religious person is that a F.A.T. Christian is humble, willing to be broken, and consistently takes steps toward walking in obedience, whereas a religious person lacks these characteristics. If our disciples show humility and a genuine desire to grow spiritually, continue giving them chances. You can discern whether their progress is authentic or not—some of us simply have more bad habits to overcome, and we are all works in progress.

7. Why is it important to clearly communicate the cost of discipleship from the beginning?

8. How can casting a clear vision help someone commit more fully to the discipleship journey?

9. What does it look like in your life to balance high standards with grace and compassion?

10. How can you tell the difference between someone who is religious and someone who is a F.A.T. (Faithful, Available, Teachable) disciple?

PRAYER

Father God, Thank You for calling me to a life of excellence and purpose in You. Help me to raise the bar in my relationship with You, not out of pride or perfectionism, but out of deep love and devotion. Give me eyes to see those who are truly seeking You and a heart of compassion for those still struggling. Teach me to lead with grace, to disciple with humility, and to live a life that reflects Your holiness. Keep me faithful, available, and teachable. May everything, I do point others to You. In Jesus' name, amen.

DEEPER THOUGHT AND DISCUSSION

In a world that often celebrates mediocrity or self-promotion, the call to live a life of excellence for God stands in stark contrast. As followers of Christ, we are not just called to be "good people" or "nice Christians"—we are called to reflect the character of Christ through a life of holiness, humility, and purpose. This means raising the bar, not just in outward behavior, but in the inward posture of our hearts.

Discipleship is not about perfection but about direction—a life that is consistently moving toward Jesus. When we seek out people to invest in, our goal isn't to find perfect individuals, but faithful, available, and teachable ones. These are people who, though broken and flawed, are willing to surrender, grow, and be transformed by God's grace.

However, in our efforts to pursue excellence, we must be careful not to fall into legalism. Raising the bar is not about becoming rigid or harsh—it's about living with intentionality and integrity, fueled by love and empowered by the Holy Spirit. A true disciple walks humbly, aware of their shortcomings, yet confident in God's ability to redeem and use them.

Personal Study Day 3

OVERVIEW:

Why would Jesus set the bar so high for His disciples if being a disciple only involved going to church and reading your Bible? Jesus sets the bar so high because He knows what He is calling us into.

Jesus came to build His kingdom and battle for the hearts of mankind. That is His mission! His method is to use us as His disciples to fulfill that mission here on earth! This is why the bar is set so high. He is looking for builders and battlers, workers, and warriors. A person is not a disciple because they go to church and read their Bible. Jesus would not say what He says in Luke 14:26-27 if that were the case. To be a disciple is to join Jesus in His mission to build His Kingdom and battle for the hearts of mankind. That is why the bar is set so high.

Joel 2:11- "The Lord thunders at the head of His army; His forces are beyond number, and mighty is the army that obeys His command."

PERSONAL APPLICATION:

<u>Key Highlight:</u>

Giving our life to a project of this size is costly. We must set aside our personal dreams, goals, and ambitions. We find ourselves in a spiritual war against the world systems that have held humanity captive since the dawn of time. Satan's forces will relentlessly fight to maintain their dominion, refusing to yield ground without a fierce battle.

As Scripture reminds us in *Ephesians 6:12, "For we do not wrestle against flesh and blood, but against the rulers, against the authorities, against the cosmic powers over this present darkness, against the spiritual forces of evil in the heavenly places."*

Going to war is risky and sacrificial. We could lose everything in the physical world! Jesus does not want half-hearted followers. If we quit halfway through the building, what does that accomplish? If we retreat at the first sign of danger, what good is that?

1. What personal dreams, goals, or ambitions might God be asking you to lay down for the sake of His Kingdom?

2. How does understanding the reality of spiritual warfare (Ephesians 6:12) shape your view of discipleship and commitment to Christ?

3. What would it look like for you to move from being a half-hearted follower to a fully committed disciple of Jesus, even when it's costly?

Key Highlight:

As warriors, we press on, determined to finish the race strong. We lay down our rights in humble submission to God's army, rejecting the standards of the world and choosing instead to abide in Jesus as our guiding light. Scripture reminds us in *Hebrews 12:1-2: "Therefore, since we are surrounded by so great a cloud of witnesses, let us also lay aside every weight, and sin which clings so closely, and let us run with endurance the race that is set before us, looking to Jesus, the founder and perfecter of our faith."* In this way, we embrace our calling with courage and conviction.

Orrin Woodward once remarked that average leaders raise the bar for themselves, good leaders raise the bar for others, but great leaders inspire others to raise their own bar. This principle should be the standard for every follower of Jesus; we are warriors called to inspire others just as He inspires us.

Dick Costolo further emphasized this point by saying, "Once in a rare while, somebody comes along who doesn't just raise the bar; they create an entirely new standard of measurement." This new standard is God's grace, transforming lives and altering everything about a person.

4. What "weights" or sins are clinging to you right now that you need to lay aside in order to run the race with endurance?

5. How does fixing your eyes on Jesus—the founder and perfecter of your faith—empower you to press on with courage?

6. What does it look like in your life to lead by example, not only through words, but by the way you live and love?

Key Highlight:

A warrior of Christ stands out from the rest, they think and act like Jesus. By setting our bar high according to God's standards, we become beacons of light in the darkness, distinguishing ourselves from the crowd. This is a standard we should all aspire to achieve.

Jesus desires to use us to accomplish extraordinary things in remarkable ways. Yet, if we have not raised the bar in our own lives to align with God's standards, we cannot effectively dream or cast vision into the lives of others. As John Quincy Adams once said, "If your actions inspire others to dream more, learn more, do more, and become more, you are a leader." This leadership is not measured by worldly standards but by God's criteria; it reflects the heart of a bond servant, one who embraces humility and service to others.

In *Matthew 20:26-28*, Jesus teaches us that *"whoever wants to become great among you must be your servant, and whoever wants to be first must be your slave."* This calling encourages us to elevate our own lives to God's standards so that we can inspire and empower others to do the same. A warrior of Jesus is strong in the Spirit and weak in the flesh.

7. What does it mean to be a true servant-leader according to Jesus' teaching in Matthew 20:26-28? How does that contrast with worldly leadership?

8. What practical steps can you take today to strengthen your spirit and weaken your flesh, becoming more like a warrior of Jesus?

PRAYER

Heavenly Father, I thank You for calling me to be a warrior for Your kingdom. Help me to raise the bar in my life according to Your standards, not the world's. Guide me to live with courage and endurance, setting aside distractions and sin that hinder my progress. Lord, teach me to serve others humbly, following the example of Jesus. May my life reflect His love and power, and may I inspire others to dream, grow, and follow You more closely. Strengthen my spirit and help me live for Your glory. In Jesus' name, Amen.

DEEPER THOUGHT AND DISCUSSION

Jesus calls us to live as warriors for Him, embracing the cost of discipleship, running the race with endurance, and leading with humility.

The Cost of Discipleship: Following Jesus isn't easy—it demands sacrifice and commitment. We're in a spiritual battle against forces of darkness, and true discipleship requires us to lay down our personal desires. This is a call to engage fully in the fight, knowing the victory is worth the cost.

Running with Endurance: We're called to persevere and run the race with purpose, keeping our eyes on Jesus. True leadership means inspiring others to raise the bar, not through our own strength, but by God's grace working in us. We don't just survive; we thrive.

Beacons of Light: As warriors, our lives should reflect Jesus' humility and service. Our actions should point others to Him, showing them the way to live with purpose. Leadership in God's kingdom is about serving others and humbling ourselves like Jesus did.

In all of this, we are not just growing in our faith but also leading others to do the same. Our lives should inspire others to follow Christ, and together, we make an impact for His Kingdom.

Personal Study Day 4

OVERVIEW:

Choosing your next disciple should come as naturally as breathing. While you must be intentional and available to disciple someone, ultimately, it is God who selects them for you. It truly hinges on your ability to walk in step with Jesus, allowing you to see and hear all that He is doing around you. A true disciple, one who possesses the ability to see others through God's eyes, will quickly identify individuals who are Faithful, Available, and Teachable (FAT). As you remain open to God's leading, like-minded people will naturally gravitate towards you.

Isaiah 30:21 -Whether you turn to the right or to the left, your ears will hear a voice behind you, saying, 'This is the way; walk in it.'

PERSONAL APPLICATION

Key Highlight:

Let's share an experience that illustrate how God is the one who selects our next disciples. In Acts 8:26-40, we read about Philip and the Ethiopian eunuch. An angel of the Lord appeared to Philip, instructing him to travel south on the road that leads from Jerusalem to Gaza, a desert area. In obedience, Philip listened. Verses 29-32 tell us that the Spirit prompted him to approach a chariot.

Philip ran to the chariot and heard the eunuch reading from the book of Isaiah. He asked, "Do you understand what you are reading?" The eunuch replied, "How can I, unless someone guides me?" Philip was available to God's leading and responded obediently to the Spirit's call. This moment was far from coincidental; Philip had to actively adjust his life to be receptive to the promptings of the Spirit. He had to physically change his location in order to fulfill God's call in that moment.

When we walk closely with Jesus, we become attuned to these divine nudges. Sometimes, we encounter potential disciples in unfamiliar circumstances or inconvenient situations, but when we follow God's lead, the results can be remarkably powerful.

1. How did Philip respond to the angel's instruction, and what does his obedience teach us about being available to God's leading?

2. Why do you think God often leads us into unfamiliar or inconvenient situations to meet potential disciples? How can we be more open to these divine appointments?

3. Reflect on a time when you felt led by God to engage with someone in an unexpected way. What was the outcome, and how did it affect your walk with God?

Key Highlight:

I would like to share a personal story about a divine appointment that unfolded during a small group study at our church. I remember attending this gathering, which included about ten different leaders, each leading their own ministries. However, I quickly realized that not all of them reflected the qualities of being Faithful, Available, and Teachable.

During our gatherings, I felt a natural outpouring of God's spirit flowing through me, urging me to speak life into those around me. As our conversations deepened, one particular pastor stood out. We connected on a spiritual level and felt a mutual call to spend more time together, encouraging one another over coffee in the weeks to come.

Through these initial meetings, it became clear that God wanted me to lead this pastor through my discipleship book, "Keys to Being Set Free." I felt compelled to share the strategies I have been learning, with the hope that this pastor could develop a personal discipleship ministry producing nine generations of disciples, just as God has done in my ministry.

I did not need to question whether this pastor was F.A.T.; the Holy Spirit inspired both of us to learn from each other in a beautiful, organic way. Our time together yielded remarkable results, allowing God to produce fruit in both of us as we became increasingly like-minded. Through God's leading we have become close friends and co-laborers in Christ. Together, we have come to understand the vital importance of surrounding ourselves with like-minded disciples who are dedicated to making disciples that make disciples. This pastor has started to implement the discipleship strategies within his church, and in chapter 11 in the book, I explore additional approaches for how other churches can begin integrating these strategies into their own ministries. *(If you're interested in more information, please see chapter 11 in the book)*

4. Reflecting on the writer's experience with this pastor, how did the Holy Spirit guide the relationship and the direction of their discipleship journey together?

5. Why is it important for discipleship relationships to be mutual, as experienced with this pastor? How does this impact the growth and fruitfulness of both individuals involved?

6. How can you apply the principles from this story in your own life, especially in your relationships with others who are pursuing spiritual growth?

Key Highlight:

Another memorable encounter happened one day at a local restaurant where I was study-ing. As I was quietly reading my Bible, a gentleman I had never met before sat down at my table without any invitation. It was clear to me that God was moving in his heart, so I introduced myself. I had not sought him out; rather, I was simply available, creating a God moment where the Holy Spirit could naturally lead him my way.

As disciples, our task is to be intentional about placing ourselves in situations where God can bring someone into our lives, if He so chooses. I must be ready and open to the op-portunities He provides. The man glanced at my Bible and asked if it was indeed a Bible I was reading, using a few colorful words to express his skepticism. Despite his vulgarity, I sensed a deeper struggle within him; this man was clearly searching and in pain.

I answered his questions genuinely and extended an invitation to meet with him again the following week so that we could get to know each other better. He eagerly accepted. Over the course of a month, I could see God working in his life as he began to embody the qualities of being Faithful, Available, and Teachable.

As we continued to meet, I initiated the opportunity for us to begin a discipleship rela-tionship. Building a genuine connection with the people God brings into our lives is vital for cultivating a thriving discipleship ministry. Always move at the pace God is working; never force discipleship onto someone. Instead, allow the Holy Spirit to open the door naturally.

After God opened the door and before we dove in, I cast a vision and made sure he un-derstood the cost of discipleship. It is essential to establish that understanding up front.

7. What does it mean to be intentional in creating opportunities for discipleship, and how can we make ourselves available for God's divine appointments?

8. Why is it important to move at the pace God is working in someone's life during a discipleship relationship, and how can we discern when it's the right time to initiate a deeper commitment to discipleship?

9. What challenges have you encountered in being open to God's leading in unexpected situations, and how can you overcome those challenges to be more available to Him?

PRAYER

Lord, thank You for the divine appointments You place in my path. Help me to be sensitive to Your Spirit, always ready and willing to follow where You lead. Make me faithful, available, and teachable—ready to connect with those You are drawing near. Give me boldness to speak life, humility to walk beside others, and wisdom to know when and how to invite them into discipleship. May I never force Your timing but always trust Your perfect plan. Use me, Lord, to raise up others who will walk closely with You. In Jesus' name, amen.

DEEPER THOUGHT AND DISCUSSION

God is the one who initiates discipleship. Whether it's through a prompting like Philip's encounter, a spiritual connection in a group setting, or a random moment in a public place—He orchestrates divine appointments. Our responsibility is to live in such a way that we're always available and willing to obey when those moments arise.

Discipleship is not about forcing relationships—it's about discerning where God is already at work and joining Him in that work. When we're tuned in to the Holy Spirit, He will highlight people who are ready and open to grow. The question is: are we ready to respond?

Let's ask ourselves: Am I positioning my life in a way that allows space for God to use me? Do I notice the people He's placing in front of me? Am I willing to go deeper, even when it's inconvenient?

These moments aren't random—they're invitations from God.

Personal Study Day 5

OVERVIEW:

God's timing is perfect, and the journey of discipleship is ongoing—not limited to our scheduled meetings. For some individuals, the cost of discipleship can be especially challenging to grasp, particularly if they have been living in rebellion for an extended period. The adjustments needed to embrace a surrendered life of excellence for Jesus can seem daunting.

Matthew 16:24 - "Whoever wants to be My disciple must deny themselves and take up their cross and follow Me."

PERSONAL APPLICATION

Key Highlight:

We are continually unlearning old habits and thank God daily for His patience with us. We must extend that same patience with grace to those whom God brings into our lives. Let us not be quick to judge; instead, let us practice longsuffering without compromising excellence. One thing is certain: God never compromises His standards or adjusts to our ways. He calls us to pursue perfection and holiness—*"Be holy, for I am holy" (1 Peter 1:16)*. He sets the bar high, and we are expected to strive for that excellent life every single day. The results are not only beautiful, reflecting Christ, but lead to a life that is fulfilled and complete, unlike anything we can experience in this world.

1. In what ways have you seen God's patience at work in your own life as you unlearn old habits?

2. How can we practically show patience and grace to others while still encouraging them to pursue excellence?

3. How can we strive for holiness and excellence without falling into legalism or self-righteousness?

4. What does it mean to practice long-suffering without compromising God's standard of holiness?

Key Highlight:

God chooses the disciples for us; our role is to be available to what He is doing around us and to respond with obedience when He brings someone into our lives. Our mission is clear: we must align ourselves with God's work and embrace the call to make disciples who will, in turn, make disciples.

Avoid the temptation to make this life all about yourself; continually surrender that mentality and remember that you're calling to disciple others never ceases. God's work is never finished as long as we are on this earth. We live for Christ, and to die is gain. But until that day comes, let us press on, set the bar high, and be intentional in our daily lives. Be available to answer the call, love people as Jesus loves them, and never give up on anyone. Stay engaged in the fight and finish strong.

5. Why is it important to continually surrender the temptation to make life about ourselves?

6. How do you personally stay motivated to "press on" and "finish strong" in your walk with Christ?

7. How can we reflect Jesus' love in our discipleship relationships, especially when it's difficult?

Key Highlight:

Follow Paul's example and be bold in your faith. He stated in *1 Corinthians 11:1, "Be imitators of me, as I am of Christ."* Paul set a high standard for himself and expected those around him to strive for the same. Such a bold proclamation can only be made when one is truly at peace with God and living a life of obedience to Jesus, guided by a clean conscience.

8. What does it take to confidently say, "Imitate me, as I imitate Christ"?

9. How can we cultivate a life that reflects bold faith like Paul's?

10. Why is a clean conscience important when leading others in discipleship?

PRAYER

Heavenly Father, Thank You for calling us to be Your disciples and to make disciples. Help us to align ourselves with Your work and to be obedient to the opportunities You bring into our lives. Give us the strength to set the bar high, pursue holiness, and love others as You do. May we follow Paul's example, boldly living out our faith with a clean conscience, reflecting Your grace in all we do. Let our lives be a testimony of Your goodness, drawing others closer to You. Guide us in staying engaged in the fight and finishing strong, for Your glory. - In Jesus' name, Amen.

DEEPER THOUGHT AND DISCUSSION:

God's call for us to make disciples is a beautiful yet challenging invitation. It requires our full surrender and availability to His timing and leading. We must resist the temptation to make life all about ourselves and instead adopt the mindset of Jesus—always looking for opportunities to serve and guide others. As we make ourselves available to God's work, we also set the bar high for the lives we lead, striving for excellence and holiness as we reflect His character.

Paul's example is a powerful reminder that we are called not just to follow Christ but to boldly lead others in the same way. The standard he set for himself is rooted in a life of obedience and peace with God—a life that aligns with Christ's teachings. As we imitate Paul's commitment, we must ask ourselves: are we living a life of such integrity and conviction that others are drawn to follow our example?

The work of making disciples is ongoing—it doesn't stop until our mission is completed. The beauty of this call is that, through our faithful obedience, we become part of God's eternal plan, impacting lives far beyond our own. Let us stay committed, setting the bar high and remaining faithful to the call, trusting God to guide us and others toward His perfect will.

Session 5 Setting the Bar High - Song

Song Title: Bar Is High

Bar Is High is a bold anthem of commitment. As disciples of Jesus, we're not called to settle for average—we're called to pursue holiness, integrity, and purpose at the highest level. Setting the bar high isn't about perfection; it's about living in a way that reflects His glory and inspires those we lead to do the same.

When we raise the standard in our lives, we show the world what it means to be set apart—fully surrendered and deeply devoted.

Bible Verse:

"Whatever you do, do it all for the glory of God." —1 Corinthians 10:31 (NIV)

♫ ♫ **Scan the QR code to listen and be challenged: raise the bar, reflect His glory, and lead with excellence.**

https://youtu.be/
dX315gqpd4g

Chapter 6

Session 6 Multiplication

To get the most out of your daily personal study, begin by reading the corresponding chapter from the book. This provides the context you will need to reflect deeply and answer the questions thoughtfully. While the study guide focuses on the first eight chapters—each divided into five sections for daily reflection—the book also includes four additional training chapters to further equip you.

Start each day in prayer, inviting the Holy Spirit to open your heart and show you what He wants you to see. As you work through the questions, do so with honesty, vulnerability, and humility. Let the Holy Spirit lead you, shape you, and bring lasting transformation through this journey.

Personal Study Day 1

OVERVIEW:

Disciple-makers, embody the characteristics of Paul described in *1 Corinthians 11:1* as they confidently invite others to *"follow them as they follow Christ."* They have a clear vision of their mission and are obedient to God in their calling. These characteristics of a disciple should be evident in all of us.

In Session 6, we will focus specifically on one key trait: a disciple multiplies themselves. This characteristic is meant to be a fundamental aspect of a disciple's life; yet, far too many in the church are not engaging in this practice. Here, we will explore some reasons why this might be occurring and envision the importance of multiplication, as well as what it can look like in a disciple's personal discipleship ministry. Later, I will cast a vision of what your discipleship ministry could look like in 10 years if you simply committed to discipling just 3 people each year; the results will blow you away.

2 Timothy 2:2(ESV): "And what you have heard from me in the presence of many witnesses entrust to faithful men who will be able to teach others also."

PERSONAL APPLICATION

Key Highlight:

Why don't we multiply? Besides our lack of intimacy with Jesus, I believe another reason many of us do not have a multiplying discipleship ministry is that we have been misled by Satan. He has convinced the church today that we are not called to be disciples like Paul, Peter, James, or John. He has led many to believe that these figures were a select group chosen for a specific time and that God is not calling all of us into full-time ministry as He did for them. As a result, we do not see it as our duty to emulate them, justifying that it is not our gift or calling to do so. This is a lie from Satan, and it is clear in the Bible that every one of us, after our conversion, is called to be multiplying disciple-makers and to engage in full-time ministry.

Paul expressed it best when he wrote that at our conversion, we become a new creation in Christ: *"The old has passed away; behold, the new has come" (2 Corinthians 5:17)*. When we walk according to the world's systems, we do not disciple because those systems control us. However, in Christ, we disciple because it is Christ's systems that guide us. Multiplying disciples is tangible evidence of the fruit of our intimate walk with God.

1. The passage says we've been misled by Satan to think we're not meant to be like Paul, Peter, James, or John. How might your perspective change if you believed you were called to the same mission?

2. The text emphasizes that every believer is called to be a multiplying disciple-maker. What are some obstacles that keep us from stepping into this role?

3. The passage contrasts walking in "the world's systems" versus "Christ's systems." What are some examples of worldly systems that hinder discipleship?

4. The passage says that multiplying disciples is "tangible evidence" of intimacy with God. How does that statement challenge or encourage you personally?

Key Highlight:

Paul instructs Timothy in *2 Timothy 4:2 to "Preach the word; be ready in season and out of season; reprove, rebuke, and exhort, with complete patience and teaching."* This calls us to be prepared disciples, regardless of whether our lives are going well or facing challenges. Too often, we create silos or separate compartments in our lives; we may behave one way at work, another at home, a different way when we are alone, and yet another at church. The Bible warns us about this in James 1:8, describing such a person as "double-minded" and "unstable in all his ways."

God reminds us that there should be no distinction in how we live as disciples. We are always representatives of Jesus, ready to be used by Him. As *Colossians 3:23-24 states: "Whatever you do, work heartily, as for the Lord and not for men, knowing that from the Lord you will receive the inheritance as your reward. You are serving the Lord Christ."* This encourages us to consistently strive for excellence in our work, as everything we do in life is ultimately an act of service to the Lord. The Bible clearly teaches that every disciple is called to engage in full-time ministry, regardless of their specific role or context.

5. 2 Timothy 4:2 urges us to be ready to preach, reprove, rebuke, and exhort "in season and out of season." What does it look like to be spiritually ready, even when life is hard or inconvenient?

6. The passage talks about creating "silos" in our lives. In what ways do people (or you personally) tend to compartmentalize their faith? Why is this dangerous for discipleship and our witness?

7. The section emphasizes that all disciples are called to full-time ministry, regardless of title or profession. What would change in your day-to-day life if you truly embraced that mindset?

Key Highlight:

Mahatma Gandhi once remarked, "I like your Christ, I do not like your Christians. Your Christians are so unlike your Christ." This statement highlights a troubling reality: many within the church seem to lack the consistent time spent in God's presence to experience His pure, undefiled love. Such love has the power to transform us, revealing the truth and dispelling Satan's lies. This clarity helps awaken our calling and ignites revival in our hearts, drawing us closer to the original disciples who were willing to risk everything for Him.

There are two types of Christians: those who seek God's hand for what He can give them and those who seek His face for an authentic relationship with Him. Few take the time to sit in His presence and simply behold His beauty. Most are preoccupied with seeking something from God. As *Psalm 27:8 says, "When You said, 'Seek My face,' my heart said to You, 'Your face, Lord, I will seek.'"* Gandhi did not encounter Christians who sought God's face, where His love flowed abundantly; instead, he met those who primarily sought His hands and what God could give them.

A disciple who seeks God's face daily rises filled with joy and ready for the challenges ahead, fully equipped for the tasks God places before them. Their love for others becomes contagious, radiating joy and purpose to those around them. The days of boredom and depression fade away, replaced by a thrilling adventure each moment brings. Their dreams shift from planning the next vacation to discovering new ways to build God's Kingdom.

8. Gandhi said, "I like your Christ, I do not like your Christians." Why do you think Ghandi thought Christians where different then Christs' teachings?

9. There is a contrast between those who seek God's hand and those who seek His face. What do you think it means to seek God's hand? What does it mean to seek His face? Which one do you tend to seek more often—and why?

10. The section describes a disciple who seeks God's face as joyful, ready, and contagious in love. What stands out to you most about that kind of life? Do you know anyone who lives like that?

11. How does seeking God's presence change our dreams, goals, and desires?

PRAYER

Lord Jesus, Thank You for calling me to be Your disciple. Help me to live boldly, not just for myself, but to multiply and lead others to You. Make me consistent in every area of my life—at home, at work, and in private. Teach me to seek Your face more than Your hand, to sit in Your presence, and to be filled with Your love. Let my life reflect You and draw others closer to Your heart. In Your name, Amen.

DEEPER THOUGHT AND DISCUSSION

At the core of discipleship is a transformed heart that overflows into a transformed life. Many Christians today struggle to multiply because they have settled for a surface-level relationship with God—one that seeks blessings more than His presence. **But true transformation begins when we consistently sit at His feet, seek His face, and live as if every moment belongs to Him**.

Personal Study Day 2

OVERVIEW:

Every time I meet with my disciples, my focus is on casting vision—I speak life into their ministries and create a vivid picture of what their multiplying ministry will look like.

That picture shares with them how the discipleship process works: they will go on to disciple someone else, and that disciple will in turn disciple another person, continuing this way through nine, ten, eleven, or even twelve generations deep, depending on how far God chooses to take their personal ministry. They understand that each generation builds upon the previous one, creating a chain of discipleship that multiplies their impact of advancing Gods Kingdom.

My friend and colleague, Steve Harris, who developed an impressive 9-step curriculum called Natural Discipleship. Within this curriculum, he articulates a compelling vision that distinguishes between the secrets of multiplication and addition.

So, what are multiplication and addition? In simple terms, the addition model encourages steady growth within the church, leading to the development of new leaders. In contrast, the multiplication model facilitates rapid expansion within a shorter timeframe by producing disciple-makers who go on to create even more disciples. This results in a powerful chain reaction of multiplying disciples, accompanied by significant spiritual growth as a byproduct. Understanding the difference between these two models is crucial for effectively casting vision with our disciples, as it helps us grasp God's command to go and make disciples who also make disciples.

Habakkuk 2:2-3 - "And the Lord answered me: 'Write the vision; make it plain on tablets, so he may run who reads it. For still the vision awaits its appointed time; it hastens to the end—it will not lie.

PERSONAL APPLICATION:

Key Highlight:

To illustrate this concept clearly, I will provide examples of what your ministry could look like in both the addition and multiplication models over a 10-year period.

Addition Model Example. Imagine you are a gifted evangelist who leads over 100,000 people to the Lord each year for 10 consecutive years. This adds up to 1 million individuals who have given their lives to Christ during this period. While this is a remarkable achievement, most evangelists I know do not disciple these individuals to become disciple-makers after their conversion. As I mentioned earlier in the book, research shows that only about 1 in 10 will take on the role of disciple-maker. This means that, out of the 1 million, approximately 100,000 are actively discipling others.

While it is clear that God can and does use the addition model to impact the world, the reality is that most individuals do not lead 100,000 people to Christ each year. Although some large ministry organizations might achieve this, the average Christian typically leads very few people to Jesus annually.

1. The example describes an evangelist leading 100,000 people to Christ annually—yet only a fraction become disciple-makers. What does this reveal about the limitations of the addition model alone?

2. According to the text, only about 1 in 10 new believers go on to disciple others. Why do you think that number is so low? What could help increase that ratio in the Church today?

3. Imagine what could happen if every believer saw themselves as a disciple-maker. What would your church, community, or friend group look like 10 years from now if everyone embraced this?

Key Highlight:

Based on my personal experiences and observations, I have noticed that among the individuals who lead people to Jesus each year, only a handful actively become disciple-makers. Furthermore, those who do not cast vision often find that many of their disciples are not engaging in making disciples that make disciples.

The current structure of the church often encourages members to invite their friends so that the pastor can share the Gospel with them. This addition model has become the preferred approach within the church today. In a study by Elmer Towns, he found that 86% of people who begin attending church or come to faith do so because someone invited them. While this is a positive finding, unfortunately, very few individuals lead others to Christ directly, and even fewer engage in discipleship themselves, which is not ideal.

The addition model has been the dominant approach in the church for many years, but its outcomes have led to only a small number of disciples who are genuinely committed to making more disciples.

4. The passage notes that many who lead people to Christ each year don't actively disciple others. What might be preventing people from engaging in discipleship after leading someone to Christ?

5. The text mentions that those who don't cast vision often find their disciples aren't multiplying. What does it mean to "cast vision" for discipleship, and why is it so crucial for multiplication?

6. Elmer Towns' study showed that 86% of people come to church because they were invited by someone. While this statistic is positive, why is it not enough for the health of the Church in the long term?

7. How do you feel about the idea of shifting the focus from inviting others to church to empowering individuals to directly share the Gospel and make disciples?

Key Highlight:

Many individuals within the church tend to seek God's assistance rather than His presence, focusing on what He can do for them rather than cultivating a deep relationship with Him. As a result, they often bring others to church in hopes they get the support for their friends, rather than actively engaging in the discipleship process themselves.

While many churches provide discipleship classes and emphasize their significance, relatively few have active members who are successfully multiplying disciples. In addition to these classes, which I refer to as our "spiritual discipline classes," we gather in small groups to cultivate greater discipline in our faith. However, this type of meeting often fails to produce multiplication of disciples in the broader community.

In essence, the addition model of the church tends to generate leaders who can lead others, but it falls short in cultivating disciples who actively make more disciples.

8. The section discusses how many Christians seek God's assistance but not His presence. What do you think is the difference between seeking God's help in times of need versus seeking a deep, ongoing relationship with Him?

9. The text refers to "spiritual discipline classes" as opportunities to cultivate greater discipline in our faith. How can small groups be better utilized to encourage not just discipline, but also active multiplication of disciples?

10. The addition model creates leaders but often fails to cultivate disciple-makers. How can we, as a Church, focus on making disciples who go on to make disciples rather than just raising leaders?

PRAYER

Father God, Thank You for calling me to be a disciple and to make disciples. Forgive me for the times I've focused more on what You can do for me than on cultivating a deep, intimate relationship with You. Help me to seek Your face, not just Your hand. Teach me to embrace my role in making disciples, not just inviting others to church but actively investing in their spiritual growth.

Lord, I ask for a shift in my heart—from a mindset of addition to one of multiplication. Fill me with the vision to see others as potential disciple-makers and equip me to walk alongside them as they grow. Let my life reflect the love and power of Your presence and empower me to live as a witness who makes disciples that make disciples.

In Jesus' name, Amen.

DEEPER THOUGHT AND DISCUSSION

True discipleship goes beyond simply bringing people to church or teaching them in classes; it's about cultivating deep, relational connections that lead to multiplication. As followers of Jesus, we're called not only to seek His help but to seek His presence, allowing that relationship to transform us into disciple-makers. When we focus on the presence of God, we begin to see that our role is not just to lead others to Jesus, but to actively walk with them as they grow and go on to disciple others.

Personal Study Day 3

OVERVIEW:

Now, let us transition to a more practical vision that aligns with the accomplishments of the early church—an approach that many followers of Christ today have overlooked. This is the fundamentals of multiplying discipleship, and I will guide you on how to initiate this type of ministry.

To keep it simple, imagine that God gives you the opportunity to disciple just three people this year. This is not a huge commitment and is an attainable goal for most people. Let us calculate the total number of disciples using a multiplying method: If you train three disciples in one year, and each of those three disciples trains three more within the same year, the total number of disciples at the end of the first year will rise to 12. I will explain how this multiplication works shortly, but for now, let us extend this model over the next 10 years, like the addition model we discussed earlier.

Matthew 28:19-20 - "Go therefore and make disciples of all nations, baptizing them in the name of the Father and of the Son and of the Holy Spirit, teaching them to observe all that I have commanded you. And behold, I am with you always, to the end of the age."

PERSONAL APPLICATION:

Key Highlight:

Year 1:

The initial disciple trains 3 people.

Those 3 people each train 3 people as well.

So, $(3 + (3 \times 3) = 3 + 9 = 12)$ total for Year 1.

Year 2:

Each of the 9 new disciples trains 3:

$(9 \times 3 = 27)$ new disciples.

Total for Year 2 = $(12 + 27 = 39)$.

Year 3:

Each of the 27 new disciples trains 3:

$(27 \times 3 = 81)$ new disciples.

Total for Year 3 = $(39 + 81 = 120)$.

Year 4:

Each of the 81 new disciples trains 3:

$(81 \times 3 = 243)$ new disciples.

Total for Year 4 = $(120 + 243 = 363)$.

Year 5:

Each of the 243 new disciples trains 3:

$(243 \times 3 = 729)$ new disciples.

Total for Year 5 = $(363 + 729 = 1{,}092)$.

Year 6:

Each of the 729 new disciple's trains 3:

$(729 \times 3 = 2{,}187)$ new disciples.

Total for Year 6 = $(1{,}092 + 2{,}187 = 3{,}279)$.

Year 7:

Each of the 2,187 new disciple's trains 3:

$(2{,}187 \times 3 = 6{,}561)$ new disciples.

Total for Year 7 = $(3{,}279 + 6{,}561 = 9{,}840)$.

Year 8:

Each of the 6,561 new disciple's trains 3:

$(6{,}561 \times 3 = 19{,}683)$ new disciples.

Total for Year 8 = $(9{,}840 + 19{,}683 = 29{,}523)$.

Year 9:

Each of the 19,683 new disciple's trains 3:

(19,683 \times 3 = 59,049) new disciples.

Total for Year 9 = (29,523 + 59,049 = 88,572).

Year 10:

Each of the 59,049 new disciple's trains 3:

(59,049 \times 3 = 177,147) new disciples.

Total for Year 10 = (88,572 + 177,147 = 265,719).

If you commit to discipling just 3 people each year and train your disciples to do the same your ministry would grow to an astonishing 265,719 individuals after 10 years. Now, consider the impact if you maintained this lifestyle for 50 years. The mathematical progression reveals rapid multiplication, resulting in a total that could easily exceed billions

1. In Year 1, the multiplication process starts with just 3 individuals. What does this reveal about the power of small, intentional actions in discipleship?

2. By Year 10, the total number of disciples grows to 265,719. How does the thought of such growth challenge or encourage you in your own discipleship journey?

3. The text suggests the potential to impact billions if this model is sustained for 50 years. How can we encourage and equip others to adopt the mindset of multiplying disciples rather than just adding converts?

Key Highlight:

The discipleship process of multiplying by 3 every year leads to exponential growth, and by Year 50, the numbers become so vast that conventional counting becomes impractical without computational tools. This model illustrates how deeply the impact of discipleship can expand over time, reaching staggering levels of influence through continuous multiplication.

Unlike the addition model, which produces leaders capable of leading others, the multiplication model far outperforms the addition model by producing disciples who make more disciples. This approach is how the early church expanded so rapidly across the world, and it is also what I have experienced in my own discipleship ministry: remarkable growth.

However, it is important to remember that this kind of expansion is not possible without prioritizing the essential principles outlined in the previous chapters.

4. The multiplication model produces disciples who make more disciples, whereas the addition model focuses on leaders leading others. Why do you think the multiplication model was so effective in the early church and can still be effective today?

5. The passage emphasizes that exponential growth through multiplication is not possible without prioritizing key principles. What principles do you believe are essential for creating a culture of multiplication in discipleship?

6. The multiplication model requires a commitment to developing disciples who, in turn, will multiply. What can you do to help the people you disciple understand their role in multiplying and making disciples themselves?

Key Highlight:

Let us review the essential steps you need to take to cultivate a personal discipleship ministry that fosters nine generations of disciples in your personal ministry in a short amount of time.

First and foremost, you must be fully surrendered to God in every aspect of your life. This means being 100% committed to your calling in full-time ministry. I am not saying that God is asking you to quit your job, although He might. However, full-time ministry is about having the mentality of being all in—completely committed to being used by God to multiply disciples. It is about always being on the lookout for the opportunities God brings into your life. Such a commitment will allow you to cultivate a happy soul, live simply with a clean conscience, see people through Jesus's eyes, and operate in obedience to the calling He has placed on your life.

Second, it is vital to become an avid student of God's Word and to explore any other areas He opens for you to study. This preparation will equip you for the daily spiritual battles you will face.

Third, set the bar high, just as Christ has done for us. A lifestyle of holiness is our calling, and we achieve this by surrounding ourselves with people who share similar goals and aspirations. Look for faithful, available, and teachable individuals who are eager to grow with you to disciple. We are selective on whom we disciple.

Fourth, cast vision every time you meet with your disciples. From the outset, let them know that as they are being discipled, they also need to be discipling someone else. Establish this as a prerequisite for meeting with potential disciples: if they are not willing to disciple someone while being discipled themselves, then refrain from pursuing their discipleship. Teach them about the principle of multiplication and emphasize that this is what God desires for their ministry.

Fifth, build a leadership team just as Jesus did. (I will elaborate on this in our next session.)

7. How can you assess whether you are truly surrendered to God in your calling, whether full-time ministry or not?

8. Why is it important to surround yourself with individuals who share your discipleship goals, and how can this impact your growth and theirs?

9. How does becoming a student of the Word prepare you for both personal growth and guiding others?

PRAYER

Lord, I surrender my life fully to You, trusting in Your guidance and calling. Help me to be all in, whether in my ministry, work, or relationships. Equip me with Your Word, strengthen my faith, and prepare me for the spiritual battles ahead. Surround me with faithful, teachable people who share a desire to grow in You.

Grant me the courage to cast vision for multiplication, teaching others the importance of discipleship and empowering them to multiply. Lead me in building a strong leadership team, following Your example of mentorship and growth. May my life reflect Your holiness and Your heart for others, as I seek to make disciples who make disciples. In Jesus' name, Amen.

DEEPER THOUGHT AND DISCUSSION

Discipleship is not just about personal growth; it's about creating a ripple effect. When we choose to multiply disciples, we align ourselves with God's ultimate plan to spread His Kingdom. This requires not just commitment to our own spiritual walk but a willingness to invest in others, to help them grow and, in turn, become disciple-makers themselves. It's a chain reaction that expands God's impact far beyond what we could accomplish alone.

Personal Study Day 4

OVERVIEW:

The foundation of a successful discipleship ministry always starts with us surrendering our lives completely over to Jesus.

Joshua 1:8 - "This Book of the Law shall not depart from your mouth, but you shall meditate on it day and night, so that you may be careful to do according to all that is written in it. For then you will make your way prosperous, and then you will have good success."

PERSONAL APPLICATION

Key Highlight: Faithful

Nothing significant happens without God's anointing upon our efforts. The strategies you have learned have been birthed in being still before God. If you do these strategies, you will have disciples who have developed nine generations of disciples, but this is not due to any remarkable achievements of your own; it is because our God is great.

1. What does it mean for you to rely on God's anointing in your ministry and discipleship efforts?

2. Why is it important to be still and wait on God before taking action, especially in discipleship?

3. How can you maintain humility and give God credit for the fruit of your discipleship efforts?

4. How does the idea of "generational discipleship" inspire you in your own walk with God?

5. Reflecting on God's greatness, how can you celebrate His work in the lives of those you disciple, even if the results aren't immediately visible?

PRAYER

Lord, I humbly acknowledge that nothing of significance happens apart from Your anointing. I ask for Your presence and power to guide my efforts in discipleship. Help me to always be still before You, listening and waiting for Your direction. I know that any growth or success is not by my strength but by Your greatness, and I give You all the glory.

May my heart remain focused on Your will, and may I always remember that it is You who produces the fruit, not my own efforts. Teach me to rely fully on You, and to trust that, through Your anointing, the generations of disciples will multiply. In Jesus' name, Amen.

DEEPER THOUGHT AND DISCUSSION

Discipleship is not about the strategies or methods we use, but about yielding ourselves to God's presence and anointing. While we may develop plans and approaches, it is God's power that transforms lives and multiplies disciples. His greatness is the driving force behind lasting impact, and we must constantly remind ourselves that without Him, our efforts would be in vain. True success in discipleship comes when we align our will with His and allow His anointing to work through us.

Personal Study Day 5

OVERVIEW:

Psalm 1:2-3 - "But his delight is in the law of the Lord, and on his law he meditates day and night. He is like a tree planted by streams of water that yields its fruit in its season, and its leaf does not wither. In all that he does, he prospers."

PERSONAL APPLICATION

Key Highlight:

Set high expectations with your disciples, emphasizing the importance of becoming disciple-makers who in turn disciple others. Make sure you cast a clear vision for them, and like many of us, we still have many years of discipleship ahead.

1. How can you ensure that your expectations are both challenging and achievable for those you disciple?

2. How can you ensure that your vision will resonate with those you disciple and inspire them to take action?

3. What are some potential challenges in holding your disciples to high standards, and how can you address them with love and patience?

4. How can you maintain a mindset of patience and endurance as you invest in the long-term process of multiplying disciples?

PRAYER

Lord, Help me to set high expectations for those I disciple, always pointing them toward the vision of becoming disciple-makers who multiply Your Kingdom. Grant me the wisdom and clarity to cast this vision with passion and conviction. As I walk alongside them, remind me that discipleship is a long-term journey, and I must be patient and faithful in the process.

Give me the strength to balance grace and accountability, nurturing their growth while holding them to the standard You set before us. May my life and my discipleship reflect Your heart for others, and may we continue to grow and multiply for Your glory. - In Jesus' name, Amen.

DEEPER THOUGHT DISCUSSION:

Setting high expectations in discipleship is not about creating unrealistic demands, but about aligning the heart of the disciple with God's call to multiply. By casting a clear vision for discipleship, we invite others to see their role in God's greater mission. Discipleship is a long-term commitment, and though the process may be slow and require endurance, it's through this journey that true transformation happens. High expectations push us to grow beyond our comfort zones, but they must always be grounded in grace, love, and the understanding that we are all on a continuous journey toward maturity in Christ.

Session 6 Multiplication - Song

Song Title: Multiply in Me

Multiply in Me is a heartfelt cry to be used by God to make disciples who make disciples. It's more than a mission—it's the heartbeat of Jesus. This song captures the surrender and passion required to live a life that multiplies His love, truth, and transformation through others.

As we pour into others, we're not just passing on knowledge—we're passing on a lifestyle of obedience and spiritual reproduction that advances God's Kingdom one soul at a time.

Bible Verse:

"Go and make disciples of all nations..." —Matthew 28:19 (NIV)

♫ ♫ **Scan the QR code to listen and make it your prayer: "Lord, let Your Kingdom multiply in me."**

https://youtu.be/
2F5k_yPT9wg

Chapter 7

Session 7 Building a Leadership Team

To get the most out of your daily personal study, begin by reading the corresponding chapter from the book. This provides the context you will need to reflect deeply and answer the questions thoughtfully. While the study guide focuses on the first eight chapters—each divided into five sections for daily reflection—the book also includes four additional training chapters to further equip you.

Start each day in prayer, inviting the Holy Spirit to open your heart and show you what He wants you to see. As you work through the questions, do so with honesty, vulnerability, and humility. Let the Holy Spirit lead you, shape you, and bring lasting transformation through this journey.

OVERVIEW:

Pew Research says that most people typically maintain about 1 to 4 close friends, reflecting relationships marked by emotional support, trust, and strong connections. However, social circles can differ dramatically depending on life stages, personality traits, and social habits, so a one-size-fits-all answer does not apply.

For many of us, our inner circles consist of a handful of very close friends, along with a wider network of acquaintances. The reality is that our current lifestyles often leave little room for adding more close relationships. As followers of Christ, we strive to look to Jesus as our model, especially in matters of friendship. We constantly reflect on what our friendships should look like, who we choose to spend our time with, and who may not be beneficial for us.

Proverbs 17:17 (NIV) - "A friend loves at all times, and a brother is born for a time of adversity."

Personal Study Day 1

PERSONAL APPLICATION

Key Highlight:

Jesus associated with a diverse range of people, from tax collectors to religious leaders, and His interactions were guided by His relationship with the Father. As *John 5:19* tells us, *"I only do what I see my Father doing,"* emphasizing that His actions were a response to God's leading. Similarly, in John 12:49, He clarifies that His teachings come directly from the Father. Jesus prioritized intimacy with God, and His closest friends were those who understood His mission and purpose. In John 15:15, He reveals that His friends are those who know the Master's business and share in His teachings.

In our relationships, we should adopt a similar perspective, recognizing that our friends have been placed in our lives for a reason. It is essential to view them through God's eyes and to love them as Christ instructed. Additionally, God may call us to distance ourselves from certain friendships that hinder our closeness with Him. As we grow in our relationship with Jesus, He will clarify who we should and should not be spending time with.

1. What stands out to you about how Jesus chose and interacted with His friends?

2. How can we begin to see our friendships through God's eyes rather than just our own preferences or comfort?

3. How can we discern whether a friendship is helping us grow closer to Jesus or pulling us away from Him?

<u>Key Highlight:</u>

So, how many friends did Jesus have? When we consider His disciples, it becomes clear that while He had a multitude of followers, the ones who were deeply connected to Him shared common goals and purpose. The Bible mentions that Jesus appointed seventy-two others to go ahead of Him into towns and places He intended to visit (Luke 10:1), indicating that He had a considerable network of friendships. Ultimately, the quality of these relationships, rather than their quantity, defines their significance.

In *Acts 1:15*, it tells us that *"Peter stood up among the brothers, numbering about 120."* This suggests that there were many more individuals who were drawn to Jesus, listening to His every word. I like to refer to these individuals as your church family; they can often be closer to you than your own blood relatives. Together, you navigate life, share vacations, and work toward the common goal of spreading the love of Jesus to those around you.

As a follower of Christ, much of your time is spent engaging with this community—whether through small group studies, mid-week Bible studies, special events, or Sunday morning services. However, amidst these friendships, it is important to ask: How many of these individuals are actively multiplying disciples who, in turn, make more disciples? How many do you influence directly? How many are on mission with you in advancing the Kingdom of God, one disciple at a time?

4. What do we learn from the way Jesus structured His relationships—from the crowds to the 72, to the 12, and then the 3 closest disciples?

5. What does your current circle of friends look like? Are there a few with whom you share deep spiritual goals and a Kingdom mindset?

6. What do you think it means to be "on mission" with others? How can we recognize or build those kinds of relationships in our lives?

7. In what ways can we encourage our friends or small group members to step into disciple-making roles?

Key Highlight:

According to the definition Jesus provides in John 15:15, a true friend is someone who participates in the Father's business and shares in His teachings. We can meet these friends anywhere, as directed by the Father—whether at church, a bar, a restaurant, a store, or even a barber shop. The key is that these are friends you influence to walk closely with Jesus, who in turn make disciples that make disciples, fulfilling the Father's business.

This does not mean that every friend you have is a direct disciple, but it does mean that they are disciple-makers who influence you as you influence them. For instance, I have pastor friends who I have not directly discipled, yet we are close because we share a common mission and mutually influence each other.

There are also friends in our lives who may not share a mission-minded focus, such as co-workers or non-Christians we encounter and socialize with. If God is leading you to spend time with them, it is not necessarily for personal gain, although He may use those relationships in that way. More importantly, this is an opportunity for you to view those friendships as a mission field. You have the potential to be an influence in their lives, with the ultimate goal of guiding them toward Jesus, leading them to become disciples who make more disciples.

8. Who are the friends in your life that influence you spiritually, and whom you also influence in return? What makes those relationships meaningful?

9. Do you have relationships with non-Christians or less mission-focused friends? How might God be calling you to view those friendships as part of your mission field?

10 How can we stay mission-minded without turning people into "projects"? What does it look like to love others while still living with a Kingdom purpose?

DEEPER THOUGHT AND DISCUSSION

Jesus didn't just surround Himself with people who agreed with Him—He intentionally spent time with both the faithful and the flawed. Yet, His inner circle was marked by intimacy, purpose, and shared mission.

Personal Study Day 2

OVERVIEW:

So, how does this relate to building a discipleship leadership team? It is crucial. Our friends become disciples through the influence we have in their lives. When we walk closely with Jesus, we gain the vision to see what He is doing around us, allowing us to discern His will and adjust our lives accordingly. These connections grow into friendships, which then evolve into discipleship, as they in turn make more disciples.

Ecclesiastes 4:9–10 (NIV) - "Two are better than one, because they have a good return for their labor: If either of them falls down, one can help the other up. But pity anyone who falls and has no one to help them up."

PERSONAL APPLICATION:

Key Highlight:

Forming a leadership team comprised of friends is a natural progression that God guides us toward, mirroring the model Jesus established with His 12 disciples. My friend and colleague Geoffrey Harris developed a curriculum titled "Keys to Building a Leadership Team," in which he emphasizes that a thriving discipleship ministry cannot exist without a strong leadership team.

A crucial element of a one-to-one disciple-making strategy is the vision to eventually multiply your personal ministry by developing a leadership team, much like Jesus did.

This approach can pave the way for a disciple-making movement that reflects the impact of Jesus' own ministry.

Building a personal ministry and multiplying oneself is a powerful concept in discipleship. Jesus serves as the perfect example of this principle in action. In Luke 6:12-16, we see Jesus' spending time alone with God on a mountainside, praying fervently throughout the night. When morning came, He called His disciples to Him and carefully selected twelve of them to become His apostles. Among them were Simon (later called Peter), Andrew, James, John, Philip, Bartholomew, Matthew, Thomas, James (son of Alphaeus), Simon (called the Zealot), Judas (son of James), and Judas Iscariot, who tragically became a traitor.

This passage shows us that Jesus understood the importance of investing in others and multiplying His ministry. By selecting and pouring into a specific group of individuals, He was able to equip and develop them into influential leaders who would continue His work long after He was gone. This intentional approach is the essence of discipleship and sets the groundwork for creating a disciple-making movement.

1. Why do you think Jesus chose to build a leadership team instead of carrying out His ministry alone? What does that say about the importance of shared leadership in discipleship?

2. What qualities do you think Jesus looked for when selecting His 12 apostles? How can we apply that discernment when developing our own teams?

3. How can prayer and time with God help shape your vision for building a team like Jesus did?

Key Highlight:

As we have discussed throughout this book, Jesus did not choose His disciples without spending time with the Father alone to pray. As Jesus has taught us throughout the gospels, spending dedicated time alone with God allows us to align our heart, mind, and purpose with His will. Through prayer, we can discern the individuals whom God is calling us to invest in, just as Jesus did with his twelve disciples, who later became His 12 Apostles.

After spending time with Jesus, how do you determine who should be in your inner circle of 12 disciples? I refer to my 12 disciples as my special force team—an elite group comprised of the best of the best. They are fully equipped to confront the enemy with great power, ensuring that victory is the ultimate outcome.

Jesus called His elite group of 12 Apostles, personally training them as His first generation of disciples. A disciple is someone who is a learner of God's ways and follows Jesus, while an apostle is uniquely sent out with the authority to preach and to make disciples who, in turn, make more disciples. The goal of this book is to cultivate apostles or special force-qualified soldiers of Jesus, who are on a mission to advance God's Kingdom globally.

4. How would you define your own "special force team"? Do you currently have people in your life who fit that role, or is God calling you to form one?

5. How intentional are you about training others to become not just followers of Jesus, but leaders who multiply disciples?

6. What might be one next step you can take to build or strengthen your own team of disciple-makers?

Key Highlight:

While all disciples have the potential to become part of an elite special force team, not all choose to pursue that path. The lie of Satan convinces many that they are not meant to be elite, leading to a corresponding lack of power within the church.

To determine who these disciples are takes discernment and happens gradually over time. Start by building up to discipling 12 individuals first, and from that group, you will begin to identify those who are meant to be in your inner circle. Just as Jesus had Peter, James, and John, you will discover individuals who share your passion for multiplying disciples and are dedicated to growing and equipping others with enthusiasm.

7. Why do you think some disciples choose to pursue a deeper, more committed path of discipleship, while others may not? How does this choice affect the power and impact of the church?

8. What are some common lies or barriers (like Satan's deception) that might hold people back from embracing their full potential in Christ? How can we combat those lies in our own lives?

9. What similarities do you see between the way Jesus identified His inner circle (Peter, James, and John) and the way we might identify leaders in our own communities?

PRAYER

Lord, Thank You for calling us into the mission of making disciples who make disciples. Help me to be intentional in building strong, Kingdom-focused relationships, just as You did with Your disciples. Grant me the wisdom to discern those You've placed around me, and the courage to invest in them with purpose and love.

As I seek to build a leadership team, may I follow Your example of prayerful discernment and patience. Help me to identify and equip those who share the passion for multiplying disciples and advancing Your Kingdom. May I remain humble and faithful in this journey, trusting You to guide me in forming an inner circle that is devoted to Your will. In Jesus' name, Amen.

DEEPER THOUGHT AND DISCUSSION

Jesus' intentional investment in His disciples shows us that leadership in God's Kingdom is about multiplication, not just addition. He didn't just gather followers; He raised up leaders who would carry on His mission long after He was gone.

Personal Study Day 3

OVERVIEW:

Your goal is not only to influence those directly under your guidance but also to empower them to lead and disciple others. By cultivating a culture of multiplication within your personal discipleship ministry, you can create a ripple effect that extends far beyond your own efforts, ultimately leading to a powerful disciple-making movement.

Isaiah 55:12 (NIV) - "You will go out in joy and be led forth in peace; the mountains and hills will burst into song before you, and all the trees of the field will clap their hands."

PERSONAL APPLICATION:

Key Highlight:

A crucial aspect of building a personal leadership team involves identifying individuals who demonstrate reliability and qualification to teach others. In 2 Timothy 2:2, the apostle Paul instructs his disciple Timothy to entrust what he has learned to reliable people who will also be qualified to teach others.

The primary quality that Paul asks Timothy to look for in a disciple is reliability. It is essential to find individuals who can be trusted to faithfully pass on the teachings and values of the ministry. While reliability is crucial, there are other qualities that are also critically important in choosing the disciples who are to be a part of your leadership team.

These qualities include a teachable and humble spirit, a strong commitment to their own personal growth and development, a genuine love for others, a passion for serving and reaching out to people, and a solid understanding of the core principles of discipleship. These qualities are important because they contribute to the disciple's ability to effectively impact others and continue the ministry's work.

1. Why do you think Paul emphasizes reliability (Faithful) as the first quality to look for in a disciple (2 Timothy 2:2)? How does reliability impact the ability to lead and teach others?

2. How can we assess whether someone is truly committed to personal growth and development? What signs might indicate that a disciple is ready to take on a leadership role?

3. How do you personally cultivate a teachable and humble spirit? What are some practical ways you can nurture these qualities in others?

4. How can you ensure that those you're training not only understand the core principles of discipleship, but also live them out effectively?

Key Highlight:

This approach to ministry, focused on discipleship and building a personal ministry, differs from a purely evangelistic approach in that it emphasizes not just reaching people with the gospel but also investing in their growth and development as followers of Jesus. While evangelism involves spreading the message of salvation, discipleship goes further by equipping and empowering individuals to become leaders and replicate their ministry.

In the verse from 2 Timothy 2:2, we can see multiple generations represented. Paul is the first generation, Timothy represents the second generation as Paul's disciple, the "reliable people" mentioned would represent the third generation, and "the others they will teach" represent subsequent generations.

This verse emphasizes the importance of multiplication and the ongoing passing on of knowledge and faith from one generation to another.

5. How does the focus on discipleship differ from a purely evangelistic approach in terms of ministry goals and long-term impact?

6. In your own life, who has invested in you spiritually in a way that equipped you for leadership or ministry? How can you now pass on that investment to others?

7. What challenges might arise when trying to implement a discipleship-focused approach that emphasizes growth and leadership, rather than just conversion? How can we overcome these challenges?

Key Highlight:

Jesus was very intentional about multiplying through His Disciples. His leadership team fulfilled His Purpose of bringing the love of His Father to all of mankind, The Great Commandment (Matthew 22:36-40), and fulfilling His Mission of having us join Him in The Great Commission, Go make Disciples of all nations. (Matthew 38:19,20) and (Acts 1:8.)

The only hope of fulfilling the Great Commission is for individual disciples to make disciples and build multiplying leadership teams by following Jesus' model. When we consider the impact Jesus' team of disciples had on the world, it becomes evident how influential they were. As mentioned above, *Acts 17:6* recounts how the disciples were described as individuals *"who had turned the world upside down."*

It is remarkable to think about how just 12 men were able to make such a dramatic impact on a global scale. In our previous chapter, we discussed the power of multiplication and how quickly we can see God using our team to advance His Kingdom. By multiplying disciples, an individual's personal ministry can have a wider and deeper impact on society as a whole.

8. What does it mean to you personally that Jesus was intentional about multiplication through His disciples?

9. What would it look like for your leadership team or small group to "turn your world upside down" in your local context? What steps could move you in that direction?

> **PRAYER**
>
> Lord Jesus, Thank You for showing us the power of intentional discipleship. You didn't just reach crowds—you raised leaders. Help me to follow Your model with humility and purpose. Teach me to love deeply, lead wisely, and multiply faithfully. Show me who to invest in and give me the courage to build a team that will carry your mission forward. May my life reflect both the Great Commandment and the Great Commission.
>
> Use me, Lord, to help turn the world upside down for Your Kingdom. Amen.

DEEPER THOUGHT AND DISCUSSION

Jesus didn't build a movement by gathering the masses—He built it by deeply investing in a few. His focus wasn't on popularity but on multiplication through intentional relationships. The world was changed not by the crowd that followed Him, but by the few who truly walked with Him, were transformed, and then went out to transform others.

Personal Study Day 4

OVERVIEW:

In our study today, we'll be diving into Geoffrey Harris' curriculum, "Keys to Building a Leadership Team." In it, he outlines four key reasons why multiplying disciples is essential to the growth and strength of any ministry. As we explore these reasons together, we'll reflect on how intentional leadership development leads to lasting Kingdom impact.

2 Timothy 2:2 (NIV) - "And the things you have heard me say in the presence of many witnesses entrust to reliable people who will also be qualified to teach others."

PERSONAL APPLICATION

Key Highlight: Faithful

Perpetuating knowledge: Multiplying disciples ensures that valuable knowledge and teachings are passed down from one generation to the next. As God leads you, you lead your disciples. By replicating your disciple-making process, you can preserve the teachings of Jesus long after you are gone, leaving a lasting legacy.

Building a sustainable movement: When disciples multiply, they can form a network of like-minded God-fearing individuals who share a common purpose or values. This network can grow and evolve into a sustainable Spiritual movement, working towards a shared goal or vision even after the original leader is no longer present.

We all have different gifts and skill sets; we are not all built the same. Our likes and dislikes can vary, our habits and approaches to situations may differ, but what remains constant is our shared foundation in the Word of God and our relationship with Jesus. As disciples of Christ, we learn to see people through His eyes. He looks beyond our quirks and differences, meeting us right where we are.

1. Why is it important to you personally that the teachings of Jesus continue beyond your lifetime? How does multiplying disciples help ensure that legacy?

2. How can we be intentional about building a spiritual movement rather than just maintaining a ministry? What are the key differences between the two?

3. How can we guard against making our disciple-making strategy dependent on one person, and instead focus on equipping others to lead when we are no longer present?

Key Highlight: Available

Addressing large-scale challenges: Multiplied disciples can work together to tackle complex challenges and make a greater impact. By empowering others to become leaders and change agents, the Holy Spirit can lead your team to address societal issues on a larger scale, bringing about meaningful and lasting change.

Personal growth and development: As a leader or mentor, multiplying disciples can enhance your own personal growth and development. Through the process of guiding and nurturing others, the Holy Spirit can refine your own knowledge, skills, and leadership abilities. It's important to note that multiplying disciples goes beyond simply increasing the number of followers. It involves investing time, effort, and resources into equipping and empowering individuals to become leaders and influencers for Jesus in their own right.

In Christ, we experience unity, as He is one with the Father (John 17:20-21). Geoffrey's four points emphasize this; in Christ, we share His truth and perpetuate knowledge of Him to our disciples, fostering a like-minded community (Philippians 2:2). By building a leadership team of aligned disciples, we create a sustainable movement of God. Together, we can face life's complex challenges and support one another through difficult times (Ecclesiastes 4:9-10).

4. What are some real-world challenges you believe a team of Spirit-led disciples could effectively address today?

5. Read John 17:20–21. How does Jesus' prayer for unity among His followers influence the way we build leadership teams today?

6. Ecclesiastes 4:9–10 highlights the strength of partnership. In what ways have you experienced the power of "two being better than one" in ministry or leadership?

Key Highlight: Teachable

What blesses us most during our meetings with disciples is witnessing how Jesus is actively teaching and shaping them. We often find ourselves learning just as much through these interactions, which is why nurturing an intimate relationship with Jesus is vital for a thriving discipleship ministry (John 15:5). When we remain connected to Him, we bear much fruit and strengthen our shared mission.

Outside of our immediate circles, we know few who intentionally prioritize building a discipleship leadership team within their personal ministries. Sadly, this focus has been overlooked by much of the Church for centuries—even though it's been in plain sight all along. As Geoffrey reminded us earlier, the benefits of cultivating such teams far outweigh the effort it takes.

7. John 15:5 speaks of abiding in Jesus to bear much fruit. How does this verse guide your approach to disciple-making and leadership?

8. Why do you think the concept of building a discipleship leadership team has been overlooked in many parts of the Church?

9. What benefits have you already experienced—or hope to experience—from committing to this leadership-building approach?

PRAYER

Lord Jesus, thank You for the gift of walking alongside others in discipleship. It humbles and blesses us to see how You are personally at work in their lives—and in ours. Help us to remain deeply connected to You, our true Vine, so that we may bear lasting fruit. Teach us to build and multiply teams of faithful leaders, not for our glory, but for the advancement of Your Kingdom. May we never lose sight of the power of Your model and the calling You've placed on our lives. Strengthen us, guide us, and use us for Your mission. Amen.

DEEPER THOUGHT AND DISCUSSION

Jesus didn't just make disciples—He built a movement by intentionally pouring into a few, who would then reach the many. His model wasn't built on crowds but on committed relationships, rooted in intimacy with the Father and a clear vision for multiplication.

Today, many churches and believers focus on programs or platforms, yet overlook the power of raising up leadership teams through relational disciple-making. What would the Church look like if we returned to Jesus' original strategy—not just making converts, but forming disciple-making leaders who abide in Him and walk in step with the Spirit?

Personal Study Day 5

OVERVIEW:

Another exciting aspect is the ability to build a leadership team comprised of disciples from around the world. For example, Geoffrey introduced me to an English-speaking pastor from Rwanda Gatungo, whom I mentioned in the first chapter.

In today's interconnected world, the possibilities for building disciples and multiplying movements have expanded greatly. With the advent of social media, texting, and video conferencing, you can now build a leadership team from all corners of the globe. These powerful tools provide you with countless opportunities to connect with and influence others like never before. These technological advancements allow you to reach people from different corners of the globe in lightning speed, enabling you to share your vision of discipleship with a wider audience.

How can you connect with people from different parts of the globe? In Geoffrey's case, he created a Facebook page to identify himself as a discipleship coach, resulting in thousands of individuals reaching out to him through messenger. It was God who led these people to him; he simply responded in obedience to what God was prompting him to do.

Our journey always begins and ends with our time spent with Jesus. Seek His face daily, and He will guide you and bring others into your life each day. I have personally embraced technology to disciple individuals worldwide. Once you take that initial step, it is as if pandora's box opens—the opportunities are limitless. I now participate in weekly Zoom calls with people from the Philippines, India, and several countries in Africa.

Colossians 1:6 - "In the same way, the gospel is bearing fruit and growing throughout the whole world—just as it has been doing among you since the day you heard it and truly understood God's grace."

PERSONAL APPLICATION

Key Highlight:

Getting to 12 disciples might take years—especially if you're looking for F.A.T. disciples (Faithful, Available, and Teachable). For some, it may happen more quickly; it really depends on how God is leading you and what your availability looks like.

Like many of you, I have a full schedule. Personally, I meet with about 3 to 5 disciples each week. For me, that feels like a lot. Some of you might meet with fewer, others with more—and that's okay. The key is making sure your walk with God remains the top priority and that you're maintaining balance in your personal and family life.

Our personal discipleship ministry is the byproduct of our relationship with God. He would never want us to neglect our families for the sake of ministry. So yes—set the bar high—but make sure it is the Holy Spirit that is leading you, not your own ambition.

Now that you have built your discipleship leadership group of 12, what is the next step? The journey continues as you build relationships and encourage one another in advancing God's kingdom. Your focus shifts toward empowering them to develop their own leadership teams.

I meet weekly with my special force teams via Zoom for about an hour, bringing everyone together. While I disciple each member one-on-one, our leadership team gathers collectively. Each week is unique, guided by the Holy Spirit, as we discuss various topics, including challenging passages from the Bible. We share stories of how God is moving in our ministries, celebrate each other's successes, pray for one another, offer encouragement, and hold each other accountable. In this way, we become a close-knit family.

Over time, some team members may leave, but you will also welcome new individuals to fill those gaps. This dynamic naturally unfolds as God leads, with the focus always remaining on growing closer to Jesus and making disciples who, in turn, make more disciples.

1. How do you balance the need for discipleship with the other demands in your life, such as family, work, and personal time?

2. How do you ensure that your intimate walk with God remains your top priority as you build a discipleship ministry?

3. How do you celebrate successes within your leadership team and ensure that everyone feels valued and encouraged in their growth?

Key Highlight:

Within your team, you will likely find at least three individuals who become part of your inner circle, much like Jesus had. These are the individuals you rely on more frequently and who join you for ministry activities outside your core twelve.

What if you have more than twelve disciples who qualify for your leadership team? Depending on your available time—keeping in mind that many of us have families to prioritize—you can create sub-committees of special forces teams. While these groups consist of highly trained disciples, they operate under the umbrella of your Alpha team and might be designated as Bravo Team, Charlie Team, Delta Team, Echo Team, and so on, each with twelve members.

You can choose to meet with these sub-teams yourself or train one of your Alpha team members to oversee them, essentially replicating what you do during your Alpha team meetings. All these groups will share the same mission: to advance the Kingdom of God, one disciple at a time.

Feel free to get creative in structuring these teams based on regions, skill sets, or other factors. Trust the Holy Spirit to guide you in this process.

Your goal is to create a movement of God that endures long after you are gone. As time progresses and life slows you down, you may find it necessary to reduce the time spent coaching new disciples. This does not mean you should stop meeting with your twelve; rather, it allows you to focus more on your existing team members.

4. If you have more than twelve disciples who are ready for leadership, how can you determine when it's time to form sub-teams?

5. How do you ensure that the mission and vision remain consistent across all your teams—even if you're not personally leading each one?

6. As life circumstances change and your capacity shifts, how do you see your leadership role evolving?

Key Highlight:

When the time is right, you will need to shift your leadership responsibility and authority to the most faithful, available, and teachable member of your team. While opportunities to disciple new individuals will continue throughout your life, there may come a point when you start introducing them to your leadership team for additional discipleship.

I practice this when I am actively discipling multiple disciples each week and lack the extra time to give them the attention they need. In such cases, I have one of my leadership team members take on the role of disciple-maker for those new individuals. This approach not only fosters their growth but also empowers your team to carry on the mission.

Jesus said in *Matthew 9:35-38* He wanted His disciples to *"go throughout all the cities and villages, teaching in their synagogues and proclaiming the gospel of the kingdom and heal-*

ing every disease and every affliction. And that when they saw the crowds they were to have compassion on them, because they were harassed and helpless, like sheep without a shepherd. Then He said to his disciples, "The harvest is plentiful, but the laborers are few; therefore, pray earnestly to the Lord of the harvest to send out laborers into his harvest."

We and our leadership teams are the laborers Jesus speaks of; we are His mighty warriors of God. Like special forces, we report in daily, prepared for battle. Building a leadership team is foundational to Jesus' ministry, and His disciples followed this model, resulting in transformative change that affected the world as we know it.

Do not underestimate the importance of making leadership team-building a priority in your personal discipleship ministry. The goal is for you to personally disciple hundreds of friends throughout your lifetime.

7. How do you know when it's time to begin transferring leadership responsibilities to someone else on your team?

8. In what ways can delegating discipleship responsibilities empower your leadership team to grow in their calling?

9. Are you praying regularly for more laborers to join the mission? How can you encourage your team to do the same?

10. What excites you about the idea of discipling hundreds of people over a lifetime?

PRAYER

Lord Jesus, Thank You for the privilege of walking with You and helping others do the same. As I build and lead my discipleship team, give me wisdom to recognize those You are raising up. Help me to lead with humility, to entrust others with responsibility, and to stay focused on Your mission. May Your Spirit guide each transition, each relationship, and each meeting. Let my leadership reflect Your love, and may the work we do together bear lasting fruit for Your Kingdom. In Your Name, Amen.

Deeper Discussion:

As disciple-makers, we are not just building relationships—we're building a legacy. One that outlives us, multiplies through others, and advances God's Kingdom long after we're gone. The true test of leadership is not how many people follow you, but how many leaders you've raised who can carry the mission forward.

Jesus modeled this by entrusting His mission to a few faithful disciples who went on to change the world. The moment we begin to release responsibility and authority to others is the moment we step into generational impact.

Session 7 Building a Leadership Team - Song

Song Title: All In for You

All In for You is a rally cry for commitment and unity. Just as Jesus handpicked and invested deeply in a few, this song calls us to build a discipleship leadership team marked by surrender, trust, and shared mission.

True impact begins when a few go all in—not for themselves, but for the glory of God. This is how Jesus started a movement—and it's how we carry it forward.

Bible Verse:

"He appointed twelve that they might be with him and that he might send them out to preach." *—Mark 3:14 (NIV)*

♫ ♫ **Scan the QR code to listen and be reminded: the mission multiplies when we go all in—together.**

https://youtu.be/
nUvzo041Xh0

Chapter 8

Session 8 Disciplers' Tool Kit

To get the most out of your daily personal study, begin by reading the corresponding chapter from the book. This provides the context you will need to reflect deeply and answer the questions thoughtfully. While the study guide focuses on the first eight chapters—each divided into five sections for daily reflection—the book also includes four additional training chapters to further equip you.

Start each day in prayer, inviting the Holy Spirit to open your heart and show you what He wants you to see. As you work through the questions, do so with honesty, vulnerability, and humility. Let the Holy Spirit lead you, shape you, and bring lasting transformation through this journey.

Personal Study Day 1

OVERVIEW:

One common area of misalignment in discipleship efforts is the approach to leadership and teaching. At times, a disciple-maker may unintentionally develop a sense of superiority, aiming to be perceived as well-informed and spiritually mature. This can lead to communication that feels condescending or overly authoritative. Rather than fostering open dialogue, the dynamic may shift toward a presentation-style interaction, where the disciple-maker assumes the role of expert and emphasizes one-way instruction. While questions may still be posed to those being discipled, the intent can often become more about verifying understanding than cultivating meaningful conversation or mutual growth.

Philippians 2:3-4 (NIV): - "Do nothing out of selfish ambition or vain conceit. Rather, in humility value others above yourselves, not looking to your own interests but each of you to the interests of the others."

PERSONAL APPLICATION

Key Highlight:

What God taught me was the importance of having authentic conversations with my disciples. I had to recognize that I was their equal and that I, too, was vulnerable in my walk with Christ. I began to respond to their questions in a way that acknowledged our shared journey. I listened intently to what they were saying, allowing God to work through them to speak into my life. Our discussions became centered on Christ, shifting the focus away from my knowledge to how I could elevate them above myself (Philippians 2:3-4).

Being vulnerable and honest with my disciples has been incredibly freeing. It reassured them that I was not concerned about their opinions of me; what mattered most was my sincerity before God and how much I valued what He thought of me. This openness fosters an environment where disciples feel free to express themselves, allowing both of us to experience healing in the love of Jesus. Unlike a presentation style of discipleship that often feels condemning and inauthentic, genuine conversations create a space for grace and growth.

1. How do I view those I disciple as equals in our shared walk with Christ, or do I struggle with a need to appear spiritually superior?

2. How comfortable am I with being vulnerable about my struggles and weaknesses when discipling others? What would hold me back?"

3. When I listen to others, do I truly make space for God to speak through them into my life? Why or why not?

Key Highlight:

A conversation unfolds as you stand beside others as equals, learning together and allowing the direction of the discussion to be guided by the Holy Spirit. In contrast, a presentation follows a structured approach, aiming to accomplish as much as possible within a given timeframe, typically featuring a clear beginning, middle, and end along with a set agenda. Conversations, on the other hand, are more fluid and adaptable, responding to the dynamics of the moment.

Jesus treated His disciples with respect and often engaged with them as equals, even though He was their teacher and held divine authority. His approach was characterized by teaching, guidance, and mentorship rather than condescension.

4. In what ways can I make room for the Holy Spirit to guide the direction of my discussions with others?

5. Am I more focused on completing an agenda or curriculum, or on responding to the real-time needs and questions of those I'm walking with?

6. What adjustments can I make to foster a more fluid, Spirit-responsive environment in my discipleship relationships?

Key Highlight:

Throughout the Gospels, Jesus asked questions, encouraged discussion, and listened to His disciples, which fostered an environment of learning and growth. For example, in Matthew 16:13-16, Jesus asks His disciples who they think He is, prompting Peter to declare His identity as the Messiah. This exchange demonstrates Jesus' willingness to engage in dialogue and draw out their thoughts and beliefs.

In *Matthew 16:17*, Jesus replied, *"Blessed are you, Simon son of Jonah, for this was not revealed to you by flesh and blood, but by my Father in heaven."* A conversational approach allows the Holy Spirit to speak, enabling both sides of the conversation to be blessed by God.

Additionally, Jesus had authority and knowledge beyond their understanding, His teaching style was relational and marked by love, encouragement, and empowerment, treating His disciples with dignity as fellow workers in the Kingdom of God.

7. In what ways can I unintentionally limit the work of the Holy Spirit by dominating the conversation?

8. Do I treat those I disciple as fellow workers in God's Kingdom, or do I unintentionally place myself above them?

PRAYER

Lord Jesus, Thank You for being the perfect example of humility, love, and relational discipleship. Forgive me for the times I've led from a place of pride or control rather than grace and dependence on You. Teach me to walk alongside others as a fellow learner, not above them, and to create space for honest, Spirit-led conversations. Help me to listen more, speak with love, and lead with the heart of a servant. May my words and actions reflect Your compassion and truth, and may every conversation I have point back to You. Amen.

DEEPER THOUGHT AND DISCUSSION

Discipleship is not about transferring information; it's about transformation through relationship. When we release the need to appear knowledgeable or in control, we create space for the Holy Spirit to work—not just in others, but in us as well. True spiritual growth happens in the context of humility, shared vulnerability, and Christ-centered conversation.

Personal Study Day 2

OVERVIEW:

Another common area of misalignment in discipleship efforts is the understanding of the complementary roles of small group studies and one-on-one discipleship in the process of multiplying disciples. While small group Bible studies are widely practiced and valued in many churches, the intentional practice of one-on-one discipleship is often overlooked or underemphasized. As a result, the strategic importance of investing in individuals who will then disciple others may be missed, limiting the potential for generational multiplication within the discipleship model.

Acts 2:42 (NIV): - "They devoted themselves to the apostles' teaching and to fellowship, to the breaking of bread and to prayer."

PERSONAL APPLICATION:

Key Highlight:

I am often asked whether small group studies can be considered a form of discipleship, and the answer is yes! As long as the group is focused on pointing people to Jesus and helping them learn to walk more intimately with Him, it absolutely qualifies as discipleship. However, it is essential to acknowledge that not everyone in those small groups may develop a deep relationship with Jesus or go on to become disciples who make disciples. I suppose I understood this concept in theory, but I never viewed the people in my Bible study group as potential multiplying disciple makers.

Small groups are primarily designed for fellowship and provide a sense of community, often with an element of accountability. In addition to regular small groups, many churches offer specialized training groups where pastors and leaders guide their congregations in deeper spiritual growth. These might include classes on discipleship, financial stewardship, marriage and family topics, spiritual disciplines, leadership development, and evangelism training, among others. While these classes do contribute to discipleship, it is worth noting again that few attendees go on to become multiplying disciple makers.

1. Do I view small group participation as part of the discipleship process, or do I treat it more as a routine gathering? Why?

2. Am I intentionally looking at the people in my small group or ministry setting as potential disciple makers? Why or why not?

3. How do I distinguish between discipleship that informs and discipleship that multiplies?

4. In what ways can training classes or small groups be structured to more effectively lead people toward becoming disciple makers?

Key Highlight:

I appreciate the fellowship found in small groups and look forward to learning and spending time with my church friends. However, I now also see these gatherings as an opportunity to identify individuals who are F.A.T.—Faithful, Available, and Teachable. This book explains the importance of recognizing these qualities in others and highlights the necessity of having a personal multiplying discipleship ministry that not only nurtures individual growth but also cultivates other disciple makers.

God has called each of us to be disciple makers, and this is best achieved through one-on-one or one-on-two interactions, while also emphasizing the need to build a leadership team, just as Jesus demonstrated.

It is crucial to remember that the church is not the only place to identify F.A.T. individuals. As you grow closer to Jesus, He will open your eyes to opportunities and connections in various places, leading you to more FAT people. Being intentional and available are two primary characteristics found in multiplying disciple-makers. While small groups play a vital role within the body of Christ, true transformation in the world occurs most often through one-on-one discipleship. That is where the real impact on advancing God's Kingdom happens.

5. How intentional am I in looking for people who are Faithful, Available, and Teachable (F.A.T) in my current circles of influence?

6. Where outside of church might God be calling me to notice and engage with potential disciple-makers?

7. What steps am I taking to personally engage in one-on-one or one-on-two discipleship relationships?

Key Highlight:

Both small group and one-on-one discipleship have vital roles within the body of Christ, helping individuals draw closer to Jesus. If you are a small group leader or teach a class at church, you are indeed a disciple maker. However, it is equally important to engage in one-on-one discipleship and develop a leadership team that fosters a spiritual movement.

To fulfill our calling to advance the Kingdom of God—in our Jerusalem, Judea, Samaria, and to the ends of the earth (Acts 1:8)—the most effective approach is to cultivate multiplying disciples through personal one-on-one interactions. But we are not just looking to create any disciples; as mentioned above, we aim to identify F.A.T. individuals—Faithful, Available, and Teachable. We set high expectations for our disciples, encouraging them not only to grow closer to Jesus but also to disciple others even as we are in the process of discipling them. Additionally, we cast vision for our disciples and train them to build their own leadership teams, furthering the movement of discipleship.

8. How can I set higher expectations for the disciples I mentor, encouraging them to not only grow closer to Jesus but also to become disciple makers themselves?

9. How am I casting vision for multiplication in my discipleship relationships, and how do I ensure that vision is shared with those I disciple?

PRAYER

Lord, Thank You for calling me to make disciples. Help me to identify and invest in those who are Faithful, Available, and Teachable. Give me the wisdom to balance small groups and one-on-one discipleship and empower me to raise up leaders who will multiply Your Kingdom. Guide me in casting vision and encouraging others to grow in their walk with You. In Jesus' name, Amen.

DEEPER THOUGHT AND DISCUSSION

Discipleship is more than just transferring knowledge—it is about cultivating relationships that lead to spiritual transformation and multiplication. Small groups play a critical role in fostering community and accountability, but true multiplication of disciples often occurs in the more personal, intentional one-on-one settings. Jesus' model of relational discipleship invites us to invest deeply in others, helping them grow in their faith while empowering them to become disciple makers themselves. The journey of discipleship is never complete without the intentional focus on raising up leaders who will continue the cycle of growth and multiplication, advancing God's Kingdom.

Personal Study Day 3

OVERVIEW:

I have always struggled to find a curriculum suitable for a new Christian to guide their disciple through the discipleship process. Let's face it, the idea of starting a personal discipleship ministry can feel daunting, especially for those who have only recently begun their Christian journey. Many people often feel inadequate about their biblical knowledge and use this as an excuse to avoid discipling others. I have tried various curriculums, as well as simply opened my Bible and had discussions with others about what we learn together.

2 Corinthians 3:5: - "Not that we are competent in ourselves to claim anything for ourselves, but our competence comes from God."

PERSONAL APPLICATION:

Key Highlight:

In my opinion, the best form of discipleship is personally opening your Bible with your disciple and studying it together. However, I realized that because I never cast vision and emphasized the importance of multiplying disciples, most of my disciples did not go on to make their own disciples using this method of discipleship.

I have discovered another reason for this, in addition to the lack of casting vision: there is often a lingering doubt among people who believe that expertise in studying the Bible is reserved for church leaders and pastors. As a result, those in the early stages of their ministry hesitate to use the bible reading method of discipleship with their own disciples. While more equipped disciples may not struggle with this, those who are less familiar with the Bible often feel uncomfortable engaging in this form of discipleship with others.

1. Do I believe that opening the Bible with someone else is a sufficient and powerful form of discipleship? Why or why not?

2. Have I ever hesitated to disciple someone because I felt unqualified or lacked biblical knowledge? How did that affect my willingness to lead?

3. How can I encourage those I disciple to overcome the mindset that Bible study is only for pastors or leaders?

4. What steps can I take to model and normalize simple, Scripture-centered discipleship in my relationships?

<u>Key Highlight:</u>

This is why I believe that a well-written, easy-to-understand curriculum can be an excellent way to help Christians feel more comfortable with discipling others. Throughout my journey, I have come across several effective discipleship ministries, such as Navigators, CRU, and Young Life, each of which offers valuable resources and tools for discipleship. I still utilize some of their materials in my toolbox for effective discipleship today.

Despite the resources I had gathered from various discipleship ministries, I continued to struggle with the challenge of making my approach transferable—something that could alleviate the fears Satan uses to discourage potential disciple makers. It was not until I was introduced to Natural Discipleship that I found what I was looking for.

This resource has been a game changer for me, providing a clear and accessible path for both new and experienced believers to engage in discipleship together. Alongside the strategies outlined in this book, I had struggled to find a curriculum that would empower new Christians to confidently replicate what I was doing with them. Fortunately, the Natural Discipleship curriculum meets that need perfectly.

5. Have I found a discipleship resource or curriculum that feels both effective and easy to share with others? If not, what challenges have I faced in finding one?

6. In what ways can a well-designed curriculum help reduce the fear or hesitation that new Christians often feel about discipling others?

7. How do I evaluate whether a discipleship tool or resource is truly transferable and empowering for others to use?

8. What fears or lies might Satan be using in my own life—or the lives of those I disciple—to hinder the multiplication of disciples?

9. Have I considered building a personal toolbox of discipleship materials I can adapt for different people and stages of spiritual growth? What might that look like?

DEEPER THOUGHT AND DISCUSSION

Discipleship doesn't require perfection or expertise—it requires availability and obedience. While opening the Bible together remains a powerful method, many believers benefit from structured, easy-to-use resources that build confidence and clarity. The true strength of any discipleship tool lies in its ability to be transferred from one disciple to another, empowering a movement of multiplication. When tools are simple and Spirit-led, they help remove barriers of fear and self-doubt, allowing everyday Christians to step boldly into the mission Jesus gave us all.

Personal Study Day 4

OVERVIEW:

As mentioned yesterday, the Natural Discipleship curriculum provides a clear and practical path for spiritual growth through its 9-Step curriculum. Alongside its other powerful tools—such as Keys to Being Set Free, Keys to Developing a Leadership Team, and Keys to a Spiritual Movement—all of which are designed to equip believers for transformation and multiplication. These resources are available for free in the app store. Even if you choose not to use this specific curriculum, it is important to find a similar format that encourages natural, Spirit-led conversation—just as the Natural Discipleship materials are designed to do.

Ephesians 4:11–12 (NIV): "So Christ himself gave the apostles, the prophets, the evangelists, the pastors and teachers, to equip his people for works of service, so that the body of Christ may be built up."

PERSONAL APPLICATION

<u>Key Highlight:</u>

Natural Discipleship offers a 9-step curriculum that has been translated into multiple languages. The curriculum is well-written and easy to understand, providing disciples with a solid foundation for their faith. It teaches them how to pray specifically for new disciples who may be right in front of them, equips them to study the Bible effectively, and prepares them for ministry. Most importantly, it is transferable, allowing a new Christian to guide another through it. All of their curriculums follow the same format, fostering conversation rather than merely presenting information.

The process for navigating the curriculum is straightforward: the disciple reads the coach's portion while their disciple reads the student portion. Each section includes discussion questions, allowing the Holy Spirit to engage with each participant. The content itself addresses all questions, alleviating the fear of not having all the answers.

It is important to remember that when following the strategies presented in this book, disciples should have a supportive team around them. This way, if any questions arise that the disciple cannot answer, someone is available to provide assistance. Each of the curriculums includes training and clearly outlines expectations, and they provide this material free of charge through their Natural Discipleship app.

1. How might using a structured curriculum like Natural Discipleship help me feel more confident in leading others spiritually?

2. Do I currently use a discipleship method that fosters conversation and mutual growth, or is it more focused on presenting information?

3. How can I take practical steps to explore or begin using the Natural Discipleship app or another similar tool this week?

Key Highlight:

The "Keys to Being Set Free" curriculum was designed to address the hidden areas of our lives. Each of us has some form of self-protection or hang-up that has penetrated the deepest parts of our souls. It tackles the "why" questions we often grapple with, such as: Why do bad things happen to good people? Why do I continue to struggle with this sin? Why is it so difficult to forgive this person? Why do I exhibit addictive behavior?

This curriculum helps individuals distinguish between religion and a genuine relationship with God. It provides clarity to see things through God's perspective and encourages people to uncover the sin that is deeply buried within their hearts. I have guided many pastors through this curriculum, and I have been profoundly moved by their testimonies—how God has illuminated sins in their lives that they were previously unaware of.

Ultimately, it leads Christians to true freedom, fostering an environment where revival and intimacy with Jesus can flourish. This curriculum is designed for everyone, not just those exhibiting outward signs of sin. The most remarkable aspect of this curriculum is that the more you guide your disciples through it, the more God will reveal new areas of sin in your own life, leading to deeper personal transformation. Natural Discipleship provides this curriculum for free in our app, and it is also available for purchase in book form on Amazon and at various bookstores.

4. How do I typically respond to "why" questions like suffering, ongoing sin struggles, or unforgiveness—and how might God be inviting me to explore these more deeply?

5. What is the difference between practicing religion and pursuing a genuine relationship with God in my life right now?

6. In what ways could guiding someone else through this curriculum also lead to further personal healing and spiritual growth in my own life?

7. Am I willing to let God use a resource like Keys to Being Set Free to bring about deeper transformation in me and those I disciple?

<u>Key Highlight:</u>

My approach is to first meet with my disciple to assess their current situation and seek God's guidance on which curriculum to start with. I prioritize establishing a genuine relationship with them before diving into either the 9-Step Curriculum or Keys to Being Set Free.

Once one of these curriculums is completed, I evaluate my disciple's progress. Depending on where they stand, I either transition to the other curriculum—whether it is the "9-Step" or "Keys to Being Set Free" —or I introduce "Keys to Building a Leadership Team". After that is completed, I guide them through "Keys to a Spiritual Movement."

Many of my disciples have either completed all four of the Natural Discipleship curriculums or are in the process of doing so. Guiding your disciples through these curriculums, along with reading this book, will help establish a thriving discipleship ministry that bears fruit throughout your life. You will find a sense of completeness and fulfillment in your ministry as you witness the advancement of the Kingdom of God, one disciple at a time.

8. Why is it important to prioritize building a genuine relationship with a disciple before diving into any specific curriculum?

9. What does a "thriving discipleship ministry" look like to me personally, and how do I measure the advancement of God's Kingdom through the work I do?

PRAYER

Lord, thank You for the resources and tools You provide for discipleship. Help me to guide others with a genuine heart, always prioritizing relationships and seeking Your guidance in every step. If you guide me to lead others through curriculums like the 9-Step process and Keys to Being Set Free, I ask that You reveal areas of growth in both my life and theirs. Grant me wisdom in knowing when to transition between teachings, and the humility to always lean on Your Spirit. May the disciples I invest in be empowered to multiply, and may Your Kingdom advance through the work we do together. In Jesus' name, Amen.

DEEPER THOUGHT AND DISCUSSION

Discipleship is more than just following a curriculum—it's about building relationships that foster growth and transformation. As we guide others through tools like the Natural Discipleship resources, we are not just imparting knowledge; we are walking alongside them, listening, and allowing the Holy Spirit to guide both of us. The goal is multiplication, not just in knowledge but in the depth of relationship and spiritual growth.

Personal Study Day 5

How often and how long should you meet with your disciples?

Colossians 1:28 – "He is the one we proclaim, admonishing and teaching everyone with all wisdom, so that we may present everyone fully mature in Christ."

PERSONAL APPLICATION

Key Highlight:

I typically meet with my disciples and leadership team once a week, dedicating about an hour to an hour and a half for each session, and sometimes a bit longer if necessary. In some cases, if our schedules allow, I meet with my disciples every other week. It truly depends on how the Holy Spirit guides your time together. It is important to listen to Him first and foremost, but for me, consistently meeting with my disciples has been the path God has directed me toward.

During our meetings, I prioritize casting vision and painting a clear picture of our direction. I never rush through our time together to cover more of the curriculum; instead, I follow the guidance of the Holy Spirit and operate at His pace. For instance, with the Keys to Being Set Free curriculum, there are times when we encounter topics that evoke a lot of emotions that need to be worked through. We should not be focusing on the clock or rushing to the next section until this process is completed. However, we also should not linger on a topic without making forward progress.

1. How do you determine the right frequency and duration for your meetings?

2. In what ways do you prioritize listening to the Holy Spirit during your discipleship sessions?

3. How do you balance guiding disciples through difficult topics without rushing, yet still making steady progress?

4. How can you create a space where your disciples feel comfortable working through emotional topics while keeping the momentum of the discipleship process?

Key Highlight:

I communicate to my disciples that our time with one curriculum could span anywhere from 4 to 6 months, and I express my desire to go through all the curriculums with them, potentially inviting them to join my leadership team. Depending on the curriculum you choose, if it is not Natural Discipleship, you will need to establish the appropriate time frames to communicate with your disciples.

I set the bar high for my disciples, encouraging them to be available and engaged. To ensure that our time together is productive, I make it a point to adjust my schedule as needed and limit any interruptions while we are meeting.

5. Why should you communicate expectations regarding the duration and commitment of a curriculum to your disciples?

6. How do you set and maintain the bar high for your disciples while ensuring they feel supported and encouraged?

7. How can you invite your disciples to take on leadership roles while guiding them through the curriculum?

Key Highlight:

This book has painted a clear picture of what it means to Rise Beyond Ordinary—to be someone who ignites a spiritual revolution in response to God's calling. We have learned that God invites each of us to know Him intimately, to love His creation, and to love the people He has made, all while making disciples who in turn make more disciples. Life becomes much simpler when we align ourselves with His perfect will. Everything around us becomes clearer as God handles the heavy lifting; we only need to follow closely behind Him. This does not mean we will not face troubles; as we learned in our previous chapters, Satan desires to destroy our lives. However, we can remain calm, filled with peace, in the midst of any storm we encounter.

Developing an intimate relationship with Jesus cultivates a clean conscience and a happy soul, allowing us to see people through His eyes. We become change agents, well-equipped to face every challenge that comes our way. **A disciple who walks closely with God becomes a powerful force against the evil that holds so many lives captive.** By understanding the importance of building a leadership team, we take back land from Satan's kingdom and advance God's Kingdom one disciple at a time.

We have a mission, and we must complete it at all costs—so help us, God. As Paul shared with us in *Philippians 3:13-14 "Brothers and sisters, I do not consider myself yet to have taken hold of it. But one thing I do: Forgetting what is behind and straining toward what is ahead, I press on toward the goal to win the prize for which God has called me heavenward in Christ Jesus."* Amen!

The Apostle Paul set the example for us to follow as warriors who are more than conquerors in Christ Jesus. We will not back down or quit; instead, we will press on and finish strong. We are God's army of disciples, equipped and ready for battle. Victory is ours, and Satan will be defeated one disciple at a time. The time is now!

8. What does it mean for you to "Rise Beyond Ordinary" in your discipleship journey?

9. Reflecting on Philippians 3:13-14, how can you press on toward the goal in your discipleship efforts despite setbacks or challenges?

10. How do you view the mission of discipleship in light of the victory we have in Christ, and what motivates you to continue in this mission?

PRAYER

Lord, Thank You for the privilege of being called to rise beyond ordinary and participate in the work of advancing Your Kingdom. Help me to stay close to You, to see others through Your eyes, and to love them deeply as You do. Strengthen me in the face of challenges, and remind me that You are always with me, guiding me through the storms.

Give me the courage to press on, to forget what lies behind, and to strain toward the goal You have set before me. Help me build a strong leadership team and raise up disciples who will carry the mission forward. May my life be a reflection of Your love and power, and may I remain steadfast in Your calling, confident that victory is already ours in Christ. In Your name, Amen.

DEEPER THOUGHT AND DISCUSSION:

In our discipleship journey, we are invited not just to grow personally, but to engage in a mission that requires deep intimacy with God and a commitment to advancing His Kingdom. The concept of "rising beyond ordinary" challenges us to move past complacency, pressing on toward the goal despite difficulties. As we walk closely with God, we become equipped to face life's challenges with peace and clarity, empowered to reach others and build leadership teams that will multiply disciples.

The true essence of discipleship lies in our willingness to keep our focus on God's call, to forget what is behind, and press forward to finish the race. The role of a disciple is not only about personal growth, but about actively participating in the spiritual revolution that God has set in motion. As we walk this path, we not only transform our own lives but impact the world one disciple at a time.

Equipped for Greater Impact:

For deeper training, read chapters 9 through 12 of the Rise Beyond Ordinary book. These chapters are not included in the study guide and offer a richer understanding of God's desires for our lives. You will explore the inspiring testimony of George Müller and gain insight into what it truly means to have a happy soul. You will also learn how your personal ministry can become part of a broader spiritual movement, much like it did in the days of the early disciples. Additionally, these chapters highlight the vital role the Church plays in discipleship, helping you see people through a renewed lens and recognize how intentional training can be woven into the life of the church.

Chapter 8 Disciplers' Toolkit - Song

Song Title: Send Me to the Ones

Send Me to the Ones is a heartfelt surrender to be used by God to reach those He's already working on. It's a prayer of availability—to see with His eyes, move with His compassion, and disciple the people He brings into your path.

Discipleship doesn't start with a platform; it starts with one willing heart, ready to pour into another. This song reminds us that the best tool a discipler has is obedience to go where the Spirit leads.

Bible Verse:

"The harvest is plentiful, but the workers are few. Ask the Lord of the harvest... to send out workers into his harvest field." —Luke 10:2 (NIV)

♫ ♫**Scan the QR code to listen and make this your prayer: "Send me to the ones who are ready, Lord—I'm all in."**

https://youtu.be/
l4d6fs6tUMw

Tips for Leading a Small Group

How to Create a Spirit-Led, Life-Giving Gathering Each Week

We chose not to include a traditional "leader's guide" with preset answers to each question because the richest part of studying this material in a group is the journey of discussion itself. While the destination matters, it is the process of discovery—guided by Scripture and conversation—that truly transforms hearts and minds. Where specific answers are necessary, we have directed you to relevant Bible passages. The answers may not always be immediately obvious, but your group will be moving in the right direction—toward deeper understanding and spiritual growth.

Ultimately, our greatest desire is not simply for right answers, but for each participant to know God intimately and walk in step with His will. As Jesus summarized in *Matthew 22:37–39, "Love the Lord your God with all your heart and with all your soul and with all your mind... and love your neighbor as yourself."* From this foundation flows our mission: to make disciples who, in turn, make disciples.

Each week's session is paired with a short video to kick off your discussion. You can find all the videos at <u>risebeyondordinary.com</u>.

OVERVIEW:

1. Pray for your group throughout the week

    · Intentionally pray for each person by name throughout the week.

- Ask the Holy Spirit to open hearts, reveal Jesus, and deepen their relationship with Him.
- Pray for spiritual breakthrough and transformation.

2. Review Your Personal Study

- Go through the week's study and highlight key insights or questions to use for the group discussion time. Encourage your group members to do the same so that when you come together, everyone will have key highlights ready to share and discuss during your group time." Review the session video on risebeyondordinary.com website before your group meets.
- Pay attention to the DEEPER THOUGHT AND DISCUSSION Topics—they often lead to the richest conversations.
- Be ready to share how God spoke to you during the week.

3. Prayer Before Your meeting

- Before each meeting, take time to quiet your heart and invite the Holy Spirit to lead—not just the discussion, but your posture as a disciple maker. Leading a group is not about having all the answers; it's about walking with others toward Jesus. Begin each week in prayer, asking God to:
  - Prepare your heart to lead with humility and love.
  - Open the hearts of your group members to receive truth and share openly.
  - Reveal His will through Scripture and discussion.
  - Create a safe and Spirit-led space where transformation can take root.

    As you reflect on the content, ask:

    Lord, how do You want to shape me through this? How can I model what it means to follow You faithfully, and how can I help others do the same?

Remember, your most powerful preparation is time spent with Jesus. When your heart is aligned with His, your leadership will overflow with grace, wisdom, and authenticity.

"Not by might nor by power, but by my Spirit," says the Lord Almighty. — Zechariah 4:6

4. **Minimize Distractions**

- Create a Focused, Welcoming Space
- Think ahead: Are the chairs arranged for easy conversation? Is the room clean, quiet, and well-lit?
- Hospitality matters. Even simple touches like offering water or snacks show people they're valued.

5. **Your goal is to help everyone focus on what truly matters:**

- Connecting with God, growing as disciples, and learning how to multiply disciples.
- Encourage Meaningful Discussion
- A healthy group has space for everyone to share and grow.

Here is how to create that environment:

- Involve Everyone - Make space for each person—whether they're extroverted or quiet—to feel safe, seen, and heard.
- Foster Participation - Invite group members to read answers or questions from their personal study. Let everyone know their input matters. Spiritual growth often happens through shared insights.
- Do not Dominate (Even as the Leader)
  - Aim to speak less than half the time. Your role is to guide, not lecture.
- Let the book's questions drive the conversation. Be flexible and Spirit-led.
- Gently steer the conversation back if it drifts off-topic.
- Let the Holy Spirit Lead. Do not rush.
  - If one question leads to deep discussion or ministry, that is a win.
  - It's okay if you don't finish every question. Be sensitive to what God is doing.
- Affirm & Build Up
  - Celebrate and affirm people's insights and encourage them.
  - Always speak life. As Jesus taught, "Whoever wants to be first must be the servant of all." Lead with humility.
- Keep the Group Connected
  - Build Community Beyond the Meeting
  - Reach out mid-week with a quick message or prayer.
  - Share a Scripture or check in on how people are doing.
  - The more connected people feel during the week, the more excited they will be to return.

Final Encouragement for Leaders

You are not just leading a group—you are creating space for people to encounter Jesus, grow in faith, and become disciple-makers. Stay rooted in prayer, lean on the Holy Spirit, and trust that God is working through you.

Example Group Session Meeting Timeline

0:00–0:15 Welcome & Fellowship (10 min)
    Casual catch-up as people arrive
    Light snacks or drinks (optional)
    Quick icebreaker or "one-word check-in" to get everyone talking

0:15–0:25 Recap & Video Reflection (up to 10 min) (find video at risebeyondordinary.com)
    Briefly recap last week's topic
    Ask 1–2 opening questions to connect the video to the book chapter
    Example: "What stood out to you from the video?" or "How did the video prepare you for this chapter?"

0:25–1:10 Book Discussion & Application (45 min)
    Dive into questions from the book or a study guide
    Encourage open discussion—no pressure to have "the right answers"
    Sample structure:
        3–5 key questions
        1 personal reflection (e.g., "How does this apply to your life this week?")
        1 group reflection (e.g., "How can we support each other in this?")

1:10–1:25 — Prayer & Wrap-Up (15 min)
    Invite prayer requests (keep it simple)
    Close in group prayer (one person or popcorn-style)
    Discuss next week's reading assignment
    Optional: End with a final question like "What's one thing you're taking away tonight?"

More from
PETE ROBERTSON

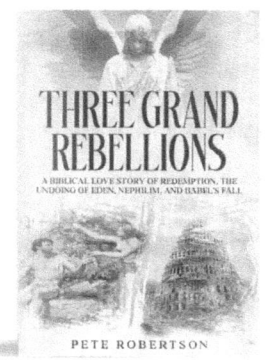

THREE GRAND REBELLIONS

15 Chapters, 179 pages

"Three Grand Rebellions: A Bible Love Story of Redemption & the Undoing of Eden, Nephilim, and Babel's Fall" is an invitation to embark on a profound journey, a quest to illuminate the subtle and profound intricacies of divine design that have too often lain concealed in the shadows of our understanding.

KEYS TO BEING SET FREE

10 Keys, 258 pages

Are you tired of being held captive by hurts, addictions, and hang-ups? Has your spiritual journey become stagnant and nearly devoid of vitality?
Do you yearn for a life of genuine freedom, where the burden of your current lifestyle no longer determines your current state? Look no further. Keys to Being Set Free is a one-on-one transformative discipleship curriculum you've been looking for.

CONQUER THROUGH SURRENDER

14 Chapters, 214 pages

A survival guide to overcoming life's toughest challengers. Learn how to thrive in adversity by overcoming obstacles and finding strength in God.in the shadows of our understanding.